the French Kitchen

the French Kitchen

MICHEL ROUX JR.

RECIPES FROM THE
MASTER OF FRENCH COOKING

weldon**owen**

Contents

the French Kitchen

In a French home, the kitchen is the heart and soul of the house. Everything happens in the kitchen — it is at the center of family life, the place where everyone cooks, eats, and gets together for celebrations, and where friends congregate for a drink and snack. For our family, as for many in France, life has always revolved around food, and I find that the tastes and smells of certain dishes evoke powerful memories of my childhood and of different times in my life like nothing else.

Food in France has always been about much more than mere sustenance. More often than not it is part of family history, with favorite recipes handed down through many generations and remembered fondly at the table. Regionality in cooking is paramount, and fiercely defended. The classics are loved, and equally sacrosanct.

I was brought up in a French household, albeit in England, and my family had that passion for good ingredients that you find only in France. My father reared rabbits, pigeons, and chickens for the table and we gathered snails and caught crayfish. In summer we searched for wild strawberries in the hedgerows, and in autumn we collected chestnuts in the woods. Fishing, hunting, and foraging were the norm and part of everyday life for us, not simply a passing fad or a fashionable term on a restaurant menu.

Our family ate traditional French food, of course, and both my parents were fantastic cooks. However busy my mother and father might have been, we sat down and shared a proper meal together as a family at the table, never in front of the television or as a rushed snack.

Many of the recipes in this book are for the dishes that I've enjoyed for years, both at home with the family and at work. They are classics and, with a few adjustments here and there, they are as popular today as they have always been. In fact, I'm often asked to explain what makes a recipe a classic, and I think the simple answer is that it is a dish that has stood the test of time. A classic can be anything from a pan of sautéed potatoes, redolent with garlic and herbs, to the most extravagant fish or meat dishes or beautiful pastries. It doesn't have to be complex or difficult to make – a perfect roast chicken, served with some morel mushrooms and creamy mashed potato can be one of the best of all meals. A classic can also be a combination of flavors that works so well that it is used in many different dishes, such as sweet and sour, or tomato and basil – such partnerships are the cornerstones of the classics.

We French take mealtimes seriously. We don't see food as mere fuel, but as something to be savored and enjoyed, and this means that you appreciate what you eat all the more. There is always a structure to a French meal, even if it is just a light lunch or family supper, and the menu will be properly balanced. There will be vegetables and salad, and there is always a beginning and an end to a meal. The food must be served properly, not just tossed on the plate. The starter may only be some salad leaves or a few radishes with butter and sea salt, the main course might even be just a plate of charcuterie, but there will be cornichons, good mustard, and of course bread – always bread. Cheese is a must for any meal, and it is the French custom to serve it with a knife and fork. Finally, there may be some fruit or yogurt – always full-fat – and coffee with a little sweet treat if no dessert. This could be a square or two of good chocolate, a little madeleine or *calison d'Aix*, or some *nougat de Montelimar*.

There are great dishes in all cuisines, but for me, the cooking of France is the best in the world. Perhaps I am biased, but in the French kitchen there is a wonderful respect for food that I admire so much. Cookery is constantly evolving and there will always be fashions and fads. But I believe that every keen cook needs to master the essential techniques and be able to roast a joint or bird on the bone, to braise, pot roast, grill, and poach, and to make a decent sauce. These are the skills that French classics are built on. I like to refer to the great masters of French cuisine – Escoffier, Carême, Boulestin, and others. Yes, they may have been working a hundred years ago or more, but interestingly enough you find that there are few techniques used today that they didn't think of first. All the things we now associate with modern cuisine, such as jellies, foams, and water baths, are not at all innovative but old skills and techniques that have simply been given a makeover.

The best recipes allow the ingredients to sing out so that their flavors can be enjoyed to the full. The skill is to respect the food, prepare it with care, and present it attractively, so that even the simplest soup or salad becomes an exquisite meal.

Embrace these classic recipes for what they are, for the skills that are needed to cook them, for the love that we have for them, and the immense pleasure they give. Here are some of my favorites.

La bonne cuisine est la base du véritable bonheur

Good food is the foundation of genuine happiness
AUGUSTE ESCOFFIER

The word *souper* means to have supper, and a good soup can indeed be the main part of a meal in France, especially in the countryside. A French soup will be wholesome with plenty of vegetables, perhaps a little meat, and, depending on the part of France, some butter, cream, or olive oil. Soups are very regional dishes, and there are many different recipes for classics such as onion soup – each claiming to be the ultimate. There are also lighter, more elegant soups such as consommés that are ideal served as a starter for a special meal.

Soupes

Crème Crécy

CREAM OF CARROT SOUP

The addition of rice to this soup makes it wonderfully creamy and smooth. Bacon fat gives a lovely depth, but you can use vegetable oil if you prefer; if you'd like to keep the soup vegetarian, make it with good vegetable stock (see page 320). There are many stories about the origin of the name of this soup, but it could be linked to the famous Battle of Crécy, fought between the French and the English in 1346. Legend has it that the battle took place on a field of carrots.

Warm the bacon fat or vegetable oil in a large saucepan over medium heat. Add the regular carrots and onion and cook gently until tender, then stir in the rice and continue to cook for 2–3 minutes. Pour in the stock and simmer until the rice is cooked, 20 minutes. Shred the heirloom carrots into thin slivers on a mandoline and set them aside.

Season the soup, then transfer it to a food processor and blitz until smooth. Tip the soup back into the pan and whisk in the butter just before serving. Add some carrot slivers to each bowl.

SERVES 6

¼ cup bacon fat or vegetable oil
1½ lb large regular carrots, peeled and finely sliced
1 white onion, peeled and finely sliced
¼ cup medium-grain rice, such as paella rice
2 quarts chicken stock (see page 320)
1 bunch of heirloom carrots (mixed colors), peeled
6 tbsp unsalted butter, diced
salt
black pepper

Biersupp et petites brochettes à la Suissesse

BEER SOUP WITH CHEESE AND HAM KEBABS

A classic recipe from the Alsace region of France, beer
soup is also popular in Germany, Holland, and Belgium.
It is absolutely delicious, I promise you, and even
non–beer drinkers will be won over. Traditional lager
works well, but you can use any beer you particularly
enjoy, including fruit-based beers. The little brochettes
are a perfect accompaniment to the soup, or can be
served as a snack or with a salad as a light lunch.

Melt the butter in a saucepan over medium heat, add the onion, and cook
until soft. When the onion is just starting to take on a little color, add the
bread crumbs and the lager. Bring to a boil and cook for 3 minutes, then
pour in the stock and continue to simmer for 20 minutes. Season with
the sugar, salt, and pepper.

Blend the soup in a food processor until smooth, then tip it back into the
pan and whisk in the crème fraîche. Sprinkle with a little grated nutmeg
before serving with the cheese and ham brochettes.

BROCHETTES

Cut each slice of ham in half and cut the cheese into oblongs of about
2 x ½ inch. Wrap a piece of ham around each piece of cheese and thread
them onto little bamboo skewers or decorative metal ones.

Spread the flour and bread crumbs on separate plates and beat the egg in a
bowl. Dust each brochette with flour, dip it into the egg, and finally coat with
bread crumbs. Half fill a heavy saucepan or deep-fat fryer with oil and heat
to 350°F, then cook the brochettes until they are golden and crispy. Drain
them on paper towels before serving. Always take care when deep-frying
food and never leave hot oil unattended.

SERVES 4

1 tbsp unsalted butter
1 onion, peeled and chopped
2 cups fresh white bread
    crumbs
1 bottle (12 fl oz) good-
    quality lager
2 cups chicken stock
    (see page 320)
2 tsp brown sugar
2 tbsp crème fraîche
freshly grated nutmeg
salt
black pepper

PETITES BROCHETTES
    À LA SUISSESSE

8 slices good-quality air-
    dried ham (not too thin)
7 oz Gruyère cheese, sliced
    ⅜ inch (1 cm) thick
2 tbsp all-purpose flour
2 tbsp bread crumbs
1 free-range egg
vegetable oil, for
    deep-frying

Crème Vichyssoise

CREAM OF LEEK AND POTATO SOUP

I have seen this soup served hot, which is totally
wrong. It should be ice cold, with little embellishment.
However, I must say that the addition of little floating
islands of crème fraîche dotted with chives does make
this great soup into something extraordinary.

Wash and trim the leeks, discarding the tough parts of the dark green leaves,
and slice them thinly. Melt the butter in a large saucepan over medium heat,
add the leeks and onions, and cook gently until translucent and tender.
Add the potatoes, 3 cups water, and the stock, then simmer for 20 minutes.
Pour in the cream and cook for a further 5 minutes.

Season the soup, then tip it into a food processor and blend until smooth.
Pass it through a fine sieve into a bowl set on ice and let chill. To serve,
sprinkle with chopped chives and some chive flowers, if available, and
drizzle on a little extra cream, if you like.

For the crème fraîche islands, stir some chopped chives into the crème
fraîche, then add small spoonfuls to the soup just before serving.

SERVES 8

1½ lb leeks
3 tbsp unsalted butter
⅔ lb white onions, peeled
    and chopped
⅔ lb potatoes, peeled and
    chopped
3 cups chicken stock
    (see page 320)
1¼ cups heavy cream,
    plus extra for serving
1 bunch of chives, chopped
    (with flowers if possible)
crème fraîche (optional)
salt
black pepper

Soupe à l'oignon Lyonnaise

LYONNAISE ONION SOUP

Filling, warming, and totally satisfying, this is one of
the most famous of all French soups and a true classic.
It's made all over the country, and almost every region
has its own version.

Melt the 4 tablespoons butter with the tablespoon of oil in a pan over
medium heat, then add the sliced onions. Cook, stirring occasionally, until
the onions caramelize and become sweet and tender – don't cover the pan.
Once the onions are ready, add the white wine and cook until the liquid
has reduced by half.

Melt the tablespoon of butter in a large saucepan over medium heat, add
the flour, and mix well to make a roux. Cook until the roux is light brown,
but don't let it burn. Pour in the beef stock, whisking well, and simmer
for 5 minutes. Add the onion mixture, season generously, and cook for
another 30 minutes. Meanwhile, toast some slices of baguette.

Preheat the broiler. Mix the egg yolks, port, and crème fraîche together
and divide the mixture among heatproof soup bowls. Pour some hot soup
into each bowl, stirring it into the egg mixture with a fork. Add some slices
of toasted baguette, sprinkle with grated Gruyère, and glaze under the hot
broiler until the cheese is golden and bubbling. Serve immediately.

SERVES 8–10

4 tbsp unsalted butter,
 plus 1 tbsp
1 tbsp vegetable oil
2 lb best-quality onions,
 peeled and sliced
1 bottle of dry white wine
1/3 cup all-purpose flour
7 cups beef stock
 (see page 323)
1 baguette, sliced
5 free-range egg yolks
6 tbsp port
8 oz crème fraîche
10 oz Gruyère cheese, grated
salt
black pepper

Potage essaü

PUY LENTIL AND PHEASANT SOUP

The French love soups, or *potages,* and each region,
even each town in some parts, has its own version of
the classics. Puy lentil soup is delicious on its own with
just a drizzle of cream and fried croutons, but to make
it even more special I like to make this soup with game
stock and serve it with little quenelles of pheasant.
It's best to use a cock pheasant, as hens are for roasting
and would be wasted for this recipe. Cock birds tend
to be tougher but cheaper.

SERVES 6

1 cock pheasant

1 free-range egg white

1½ cups heavy cream

freshly grated nutmeg

1 tbsp vegetable oil

1 onion, peeled and chopped

1 carrot, peeled and chopped

1 sprig of thyme

2 bay leaves

3 oz smoked bacon, sliced
   very thin (keep any
   trimmings)

1⅓ cup puy lentils, washed

salt

black pepper

Remove the breasts from the pheasant and trim off any skin and sinew.
Place the breasts in a blender with the egg white and blitz until smooth.
Pass the mixture through a fine sieve into a bowl set over ice, then beat
in 1 cup of the cream. Season with salt, pepper, and a grating of nutmeg,
then set aside.

Chop up the legs and carcass of the pheasant. Heat the vegetable oil in a
large pan over medium-high heat, add the pheasant bones, and fry until
they are just starting to caramelize. Add the onion, carrot, thyme, and bay
leaves to the pan, cook for 5 minutes, then cover with 3 quarts cold water
and add any bacon trimmings. Simmer for an hour to make a stock, then
pass the stock through a sieve.

Put the lentils into a clean pan, add 2 quarts of the pheasant stock, and
simmer until tender, 20–30 minutes. Remove a few spoonfuls of lentils
and set them aside to use as a garnish, then blitz the rest of the soup with
the remaining cream until smooth. Season with salt and pepper.

Heat the remaining stock in a pan. Shape the pheasant breast mixture into
neat quenelles (egg-shaped spoonfuls), add them to the stock, a few at a
time, and poach for 3 minutes. Broil the bacon slices until crisp.

To serve, place some cooked lentils in each bowl, add a couple of pheasant
quenelles and a slice of crispy bacon, then pour in some hot soup.

Soupe à l'ail et aux amandes

WHITE ALMOND AND GARLIC SOUP

This wonderfully summery cold soup comes from the Basque region of southwest France. An essential ingredient is *piment d'Espelette,* a smoky hot spice made from dried chile peppers and produced only in this area. The little corn and smoked duck cakes are optional, but they do add delicious flavor and texture.

Purée the chopped garlic with the egg yolk in a mini blender or food processor. Start adding the oil, a little at a time, to make a garlic mayonnaise. Scrape this into a bowl.

Put the bread and ground almonds in a food processor, add 3⅓ cups water, and blitz thoroughly until really smooth. Tip this into a bowl, stir in the garlic mayonnaise and vinegar, then season. Chill for at least 4 hours.

Serve the soup cold, garnished with a little olive oil and a sprinkling of piment d'Espelette. Add some garlic croutons if you like (see page 339) or serve with some corn and smoked duck cake.

CORN AND SMOKED DUCK CAKE

You can use a cake pan for making this or a silicone cake pop cold, which will give you 20 little balls of cake.

Preheat the oven to 400°F. Whisk the eggs, add the polenta and baking powder, then fold in the rest of the ingredients. Transfer the mixture to your cake pan or mold. If making one large cake, cook it until a skewer inserted in the center comes out clean, about 30 minutes. If making small balls of cake, cook them for about 10 minutes. Remove from the pan or molds, cut into small pieces if you've made a large cake, and serve with the soup.

SERVES 6

4 new-season garlic cloves, roughly chopped

1 free-range egg yolk

⅔ cup grapeseed oil

3 slices of day-old white bread

9 oz ground almonds

1 tbsp sherry vinegar (or more to taste)

olive oil

ground piment d'Espelette (chile powder)

salt

white pepper

CORN AND SMOKED DUCK CAKE

6 free-range eggs

1 cup plus 3 tbsp polenta

1 tsp baking powder

4 oz smoked duck, diced

1 cup corn kernels (canned are fine)

3 tbsp tomato paste

6 tbsp unsalted butter

6 tbsp heavy cream

pinch saffron strands

salt

black pepper

Si un seul élément de la cuisine Française peut être appelé important, fondamental et essentiel, cet élément est la soupe

If any one element of French cooking can be called important, basic, and essential, that element is soup

LOUIS DIAT

L'aigo boulido

GARLIC AND SAGE SOUP

L'aigo boulido means "boiled garlic" in the Provençal dialect, and this soup is often prescribed for people who are feeling under the weather or in need of some detox. It is enhanced by a touch of sage, which is also a mild antiseptic and helps the digestion. There are many variations, but everyone agrees that this is best made with new-season garlic, which is sweet and innocuous.

SERVES 4

20 new-season garlic cloves, or more to taste
pinch coarse sea salt
8 sage leaves, sliced
thick slices of stale country-style bread
2 tbsp strong olive oil (optional)

Peel the garlic and cut each clove into 5 or 6 slices. Put the garlic into a saucepan with 1 quart water and some salt, bring to a boil, and simmer for 30 minutes. Add the sage leaves and take the pan off the heat.

Tradition has it that you put the stale bread in the bottom of the bowl and pour the piping hot soup on top, with or without a drizzle of olive oil. When you've eaten all but a few spoonfuls of soup, add a dose of wine to your bowl before finishing it off – strictly medicinal of course!

Velouté de chataignes

CHESTNUT AND APPLE SOUP

A great winter warmer, this soup is a speciality of the Cévennes region of France, where chestnut trees grow in abundance. They also make a version in Corsica, where they have a thriving chestnut industry. The soup is best made with dried chestnuts, which are sold peeled and ready to reconstitute in water before being cooked.

SERVES 4

6 oz dried chestnuts
1 sprig of thyme
2 bay leaves
1 white onion, peeled and chopped
3⅓ cups vegetable stock (see page 320)
1 red apple
1 green apple
1 tbsp unsalted butter
½ tbsp superfine sugar
olive oil (optional)
salt
black pepper

Soak the chestnuts in water until reconstituted, 3–4 hours, then drain and rinse. Put the chestnuts in a large saucepan with the thyme, bay leaves, onion, and vegetable stock. Roughly chop half the red and half the green apple and add them to the pan. Bring the soup to a boil, then simmer gently until the chestnuts are tender and cooked, about 40 minutes. Take out some cooked chestnuts to use as a garnish, remove the thyme and bay leaves, then blitz the soup in a blender or food processor until smooth. Season with salt and pepper to taste.

Using a melon baller, scoop out little balls of apple from the remaining halves. Melt the butter in a small pan, add the apple balls, and sprinkle them with the sugar. Toss briefly until lightly glazed.

To serve, put a few cooked chestnuts and apple balls in each bowl, pour in some soup, then drizzle with a little olive oil, if you like.

Soupe aux abattis

GIBLET SOUP

Tasty, warming, and filling, this soup is made with parts of the chicken that some people would throw away. Not in France, though! We like to use every bit of the bird.

Cut each chicken neck into 3 pieces and the gizzards in half. Trim the thickest part of each wing to reveal the bone by pushing down the meat so it resembles a lollipop, and keep these for later. Trim the rest of the giblets as necessary.

Heat a tablespoon of the butter with a little drizzle of oil in a large saucepan and fry the necks, gizzards, wing tips, and combs. Sprinkle in the flour and stir well until brown, then pour in the stock and 2 cups water. Add the bouquet garni and seasoning and simmer until all the meat is tender, about 1 hour. Pass the soup through a strainer and keep warm.

Pick the meat off the necks and slice the gizzards and combs. Heat a tablespoon of butter in a small pan over medium heat and gently cook the sliced celery until tender. Fry the livers, hearts, and wing lollipops in the rest of the butter and a little oil until golden, then season.

Add the cooked rice to the soup and warm through. Serve the soup in deep plates with the roughly chopped meat.

SERVES 6

3 chicken necks, skinned
3 chicken gizzards
6 chicken wings,
   including tips
6 cockscombs
6 chicken livers
6 chicken hearts
3 tbsp unsalted butter
olive oil
1 tbsp all-purpose flour
1 quart chicken stock
   (see page 320)
1 bouquet garni, made up of
   thyme, bay leaf, parsley
   stalks and rosemary
   (see page 342)
2 celery ribs, sliced
3 tbsp cooked long-grain rice
salt
black pepper

Soupe de lièvre

HARE SOUP

Even non–game lovers will enjoy this meaty, wholesome soup. Some versions contain barley, but I think that the dumplings hit the spot and make this soup a hearty meal in itself.

Season the hare meat. Heat a tablespoon of oil in a large saucepan over high heat and brown all the meat, except the heart and liver. Lower the heat, add the carrot, celery, onion, bacon, and potato, and cook gently for 10 minutes. Add the bouquet garni and the stock, then simmer very gently for 2 hours – the soup should barely bubble. Skim the surface regularly and top up with hot water if necessary.

Take out the hare leg, strip off the meat, and dice it. Put this in a bowl with a little of the soup to keep it warm and moist, and set aside. Add the liver and heart to the pan and simmer the soup for another 20 minutes. Strain the soup through a fine sieve, then pick off as much meat from the bones as you can. Purée the meat, heart, and liver with a drop of the soup and keep warm.

Bring the soup back to a boil, then whisk in the cold butter, puréed meat, and the port. Serve in bowls with the diced leg meat and dumplings.

DUMPLINGS
Put the flour, suet, and seasoning in a bowl and gradually bring them together with 2 tablespoons cold water. Add the chopped parsley and knead the dough like bread until it is soft but not sticky.

Let the dough rest in the fridge for 20 minutes, then roll it into bite-sized balls. Bring a pan of salted water to a boil, drop in the dumplings, and cook until swollen, 7–8 minutes.

SERVES 4

2 shoulders, neck and ribcage of a hare
1 hare's leg
1 hare's heart and liver
vegetable oil
1 carrot, peeled and chopped
1 celery rib, chopped
1 white onion, peeled and chopped
1 slice smoked bacon, chopped (about 1 oz)
1 potato, peeled and chopped
1 bouquet garni, made up of thyme, bay leaf, parsley stalks and rosemary (see page 342)
2 quarts chicken stock (see page 320)
2 tbsp cold unsalted butter
4 tbsp port
salt
black pepper

DUMPLINGS
$7/8$ cup self-rising flour
2 oz suet
2 tbsp chopped flat-leaf parsley
salt
black pepper

Consommé de boeuf à la royale

BEEF CONSOMMÉ WITH ROYAL GARNISH

Gold leaf is the classic garnish for this – the "royale" touch on top of the little custards served in the consommé. And if you really want to gild the lily you could add a teaspoon of caviar. This is the sheer opulence and decadence of yesteryear – consommé taken to the ultimate level. You'll need little glass serving bowls to set this glorious dish off to perfection.

First prepare the custards for the garnish. Preheat the oven to 250°F and butter 4 small dariole molds measuring 2 x 2 inches. Place the molds on a baking sheet. Mix the egg yolks with the cream and season well with salt, pepper, and a grating of nutmeg, then gently pour the mixture into the molds. Cover with foil and steam the custards until they are set, 10 minutes. Let rest for 10 minutes before taking the custards out of their molds.

Trim the beef of all fat and sinew and chop the meat as finely as you can. Finely chop the vegetables, then mix them with the egg whites and a generous splash of Madeira. Tip all this into a heavy-bottomed saucepan, add the cold stock, and place over high heat. Using a spatula, stir the stock gently until it begins to simmer, then stop stirring and let cook slowly until a crust starts to form – this crust lifts all the impurities out of the stock to leave it beautifully clear. Continue to simmer for 20 minutes, then gently strain the stock through cheesecloth and check for seasoning.

Using a melon baller, make little balls from the zucchini, celery root, and carrot. Blanch them briefly in boiling salted water until al dente, then drain and plunge the balls into iced water.

To serve, delicately place a custard in the base of each glass serving bowl and top with a piece of gold leaf. Add a few of the vegetable "pearls," then pour in the hot consommé to come halfway up the custard. Serve at once.

SERVES 4

4 oz lean beef, such as skirt or shin
1 small carrot, peeled
1 shallot, peeled
½ white leek, cleaned
1 tomato, peeled
4 button mushrooms, wiped
1 celery rib
½ beet, peeled
3 free-range egg whites
splash of Madeira wine
4 quarts cold beef stock (see page 323)
salt
black pepper

ROYAL GARNISH

unsalted butter, for greasing
3 free-range egg yolks
⅔ cup light cream
freshly grated nutmeg
1 zucchini
½ celery root
1 carrot
4 pieces edible gold leaf
salt
white pepper

Soupe de moules

MUSSEL SOUP

Mussels are plentiful, cheap, and quick and easy
to prepare. The deep-fried breaded mussels I suggest
below make a great snack on their own, but they
really do make this simple soup into something
special – a meal in itself.

Wash the mussels well and scrub off any beards or barnacles. Heat a
tablespoon of the oil in a large pan over medium heat and gently cook the
chopped shallots until soft. Add the mussels, bouquet garni, and white
wine, put a lid on the pan, and cook over high heat until the mussels have
opened. Discard any that do not open. Tip the mussels into a colander
over a bowl to collect the cooking liquor, then pass the liquor through
a fine sieve and keep it for later.

Pick out the mussel meat from the shells and set aside about a quarter
of them to make breaded mussels for the garnish.

Add the remaining oil to a clean pan and sweat the carrots, celery, potato,
and leek until tender. Add the chopped tomatoes and saffron and cook for
a further 5 minutes, then add the mussel liquor and fish stock, followed by
the mussel meat. Simmer for 10 minutes, then blitz in a food processor until
smooth. Pass the soup through a fine sieve and season with salt and pepper.

Now prepare the garnish. Slice the carrot and leek on a mandoline or
cut them into fine strips. For the breaded mussels, half fill a large heavy
saucepan or a deep-fat fryer with vegetable oil and heat to 350°F. Dredge
the mussels in the seasoned flour, then dip them into the beaten egg and
coat in bread crumbs. Deep-fry the breaded mussels in batches until they
are crispy and golden.

Serve the soup with fried breaded mussels, strips of leek and carrot, and
a swirl of crème fraîche.

SERVES 8

10 lb mussels
3 tbsp vegetable oil
4 shallots, coarsely chopped
1 bouquet garni, made up of
    thyme, bay leaf and parsley
    stalks (see page 342)
1 bottle dry white wine
2 carrots, peeled and
    chopped
2 celery ribs, chopped
1 large potato, peeled
    and chopped
1 small leek, cleaned
    and chopped
8 tomatoes, chopped
pinch saffron strands
3 quarts fish stock
    (see page 324)
salt
black pepper

GARNISH

1 carrot, peeled
1 leek, cleaned
vegetable oil
1 cup plus 3 tbsp all-purpose
    flour, seasoned with salt
    and pepper
1 free-range egg, beaten
1 cup bread crumbs
crème fraîche

Velouté de coquillages

SHELLFISH SOUP

Velouté means "velvety" in French, and that is the texture this soup should have. You can adapt the recipe for different shellfish, according to what is available and your preferences, but do always include mussels and clams, as they are the base of the soup. Whelks, scallops, and lobster also work really well.

Scrub the mussels, cockles, and clams in cold water. Trim and clean the squid, removing the "beak" and innards from each one – or ask your fishmonger to do this for you. Slice the bodies into rounds and keep the bunches of tentacles whole. Peel the langoustines and discard their shells.

Put the clams and mussels in separate pans over high heat, dividing the wine equally between each pan. Cover and let cook for 4–6 minutes, depending on the size of the shellfish, then drain and keep the juices. Be careful not to overcook them or they will go chewy. Sear the squid in a very hot pan for 30 seconds.

Pick out the meat from the clams and mussels and divide this and the rest of the seafood among the soup bowls. Strain the juice through a fine sieve into a pan and place it over high heat. When it boils, add the heavy cream and crème fraîche and bring it just back to a boil. Season well and add the lemon juice, then pour the hot soup over the clams and the rest of the seafood. Grate a little nutmeg on top and serve immediately.

SERVES 6

1 lb mussels
1 lb cockles
1 lb surf clams
6 baby squid
6 cooked langoustines
1 bottle of dry champagne
   or white wine
4 oz cooked peeled brown
   shrimp
1¼ cups heavy cream
8 oz crème fraîche
juice of 2 lemons
freshly grated nutmeg
salt
black pepper

Soupe d'étrilles

BRITTANY VELVET CRAB SOUP

I remember an old Brittany saying that goes something like this: "When God made sole, the devil made skate, and when God made lobster, the devil responded with crab." That's certainly not my opinion. Although the little velvet crabs that live on the coast and in rock pools have little or no meat to be picked, their flavor is intense and sweet – perfect for this classic soup. You can kill the crabs painlessly by putting them into the freezer for an hour; they just go to sleep.

Rinse the crabs in cold water. Heat the oil in a large saucepan over medium heat, add the onions, and cook them until soft. Turn up the heat and add the crabs, stirring them around in the pan until they turn red. Using a rolling pin or meat mallet, crush and break up the crabs in the pan.

Add the saffron, bouquet garni, garlic cloves, half the tomatoes, and some seasoning. Pour in enough water to cover everything well and bring it to a boil. Skim any scum off the surface, then simmer the soup for 30 minutes.

Remove the pan from the heat and strain the soup through a metal colander into a large bowl, pressing it carefully to extract all the flavorful juices from the crabs. Then pass it through a fine sieve into a clean saucepan.

Put the potatoes in a pan of water with the seaweed, bring it to a boil, and cook until just tender. While the potatoes are cooking, toast some thin baguette slices in the oven. Drain, then peel and dice the potatoes. Cut the remaining tomatoes into small dice.

Warm the soup through in the pan, then stir in the crème fraîche and check the seasoning. Put some diced potato and tomato in each bowl, then pour in the soup and serve with toasted baguette slices. Alternatively, you can serve with fried, garlic-rubbed croutons and cheese – but a purist would not approve of such frivolity.

SERVES 6

8 lb velvet crabs or
    soft-shell crabs
2 tbsp vegetable oil
4 onions, peeled and sliced
2 pinches saffron strands
1 bouquet garni, made up of
    thyme, bay leaf, parsley
    stalks, celery, and leek
    (see page 342)
4 garlic cloves, crushed
12 ripe tomatoes, peeled
    and seeded
6 potatoes, washed (yellow-
    or red-skinned are best)
7 oz seaweed (dulse or
    kombu)
4 tbsp crème fraîche
1 baguette
salt
black pepper

A terrine or a pâté can be a homely, rustic dish —
something to have in the fridge ready for everyone to
help themselves — or the most sophisticated, elegant
creation. Some do take a bit of time and effort, but
they are satisfying to make, keep well, and serve
lots of people. These are perfect sharing dishes —
something to put on the table and enjoy with friends.
A terrine is defined by its long, loaf-like shape, and
can be made out of almost anything. A pâté, though,
is invariably made of meat, and is more often than
not pork based, as it is pork fat that gives pâté its
hallmark richness.

Terrines et pâtés

Marbré d'automne

AUTUMN MARBLED TERRINE

We love making terrines at the restaurant, and we've been serving this one since the early nineties. Full of rich flavors, it never disappoints, and it's perfectly possible to make at home too. All the ingredients are readily available, and it is really impressive. You'll need a terrine dish measuring about 10 by 3 inches, or you could use a loaf pan. I like to use black trompettes for their color, but any good wild mushrooms will do. This terrine keeps well in the fridge for about a week.

Separate the cabbage leaves, discarding the toughest and any that are damaged. Trim out the stalks and wash the leaves well. Bring a pan of salted water to a boil, add the leaves, and cook until tender. Drain, then refresh the leaves in iced water to stop the cooking, and drain again. Set aside.

Season the chicken. Heat a tablespoon of the duck fat in a frying pan over high heat and sear the chicken on both sides. Add the port, cover the chicken with a piece of parchment paper, and simmer gently until cooked. Remove the chicken and set aside, keeping the liquid. Soak the gelatin sheets in a dish of cold water to soften. Remove, squeeze out the excess water and add the softened gelatin to the pan with the port. Stir until it has dissolved, then set aside.

Heat another tablespoon of duck fat in a large pan and add the cabbage leaves. Season with salt and pepper, add the sage, and cook the cabbage until soft. Pour in the port and gelatin mixture.

Melt the remaining tablespoon of duck fat in a frying pan and sauté the mushrooms until tender. Season and set aside. Remove the skin from the smoked duck breasts and cut them into fine strips.

Line the terrine dish with plastic wrap and place a layer of port-soaked cabbage in the bottom. Now add a layer of mushrooms, more cabbage, then chicken, mushrooms, duck, cabbage, and mushrooms. Finish with a layer of cabbage leaves. Wrap the plastic wrap tightly over the top and add a weight on top to press the terrine down. Place the dish in the fridge overnight to set. The next day, use the plastic wrap to help you lift the terrine carefully out of the dish. Slice and eat with toast or garnish beautifully and serve with truffle dressing (see page 233) or herb mayonnaise (see page 333).

SERVES 12

1 Savoy cabbage
2 boneless, skinless free-range chicken half-breasts
3 tbsp duck fat
¾ cup port
5 gelatin sheets
24 sage leaves
10 oz wild mushrooms, wiped or washed and any grit removed
2 smoked duck breasts
toast, for serving – or try truffle dressing (see page 233) or herb mayonnaise (see page 333)
salt
black pepper

Boudin noir

FRENCH BLACK PUDDING

At first glance, this recipe might appear daunting but there is nothing very difficult and the result is so delicious it is well worth the effort. It does make a large amount, but the boudin freezes well. A good butcher will be able to supply the pig's head and blood, and most Italian delis stock *lardo.* If using sausage casings, buy the large size. I recommend serving it with crispy pork skin (below) and spicy tomato chutney (see page 337).

To cook the lardo, wrap it in foil and bake at the lowest possible setting in your oven for 1½ hours. Let cool, then chill and dice. Cut the cooked pig's head and tongues into ⅜- to ¾-inch dice – use everything, the ears, skin, the lot – then mix it all with the diced lardo in a bowl. Melt the duck fat in a frying pan and gently cook the diced onions until very soft and thoroughly cooked. Add them to the meat and lardo, mix in the pig's blood, spices, 2 teaspoons salt, and the cream, then the herbs, egg whites, and vinegar.

You can cook the boudin in terrines or in natural sausage casings. If using terrines, you'll need about 4, each measuring about 9 x 3½ inches. Grease them well, then spoon in the mixture and cover with greased paper and foil. Place them in a roasting pan, pour in boiling water to come about halfway up the sides, then bake in a cool oven, at 250°F until set, about 2 hours. Let cool, then chill until needed. If using casings, roll the mixture into large sausages, about 2½ inches in diameter. Tie a knot in one end of each casing, fill them, and tie securely. Bring a pan of salted water to a gentle simmer and poach the boudins for about an hour.

To serve, slice the boudin, dust with flour, and pan-fry in a little olive oil. Serve with crispy pork skin.

CRISPY PORK SKIN

Make lots of holes all over the skin with a fork, then sprinkle with lots of salt and set aside for an hour. Put the skin in a large pan of water, bring to a boil, then simmer until the skin is tender and can be pierced easily with a knife, a couple of hours. Remove it and, when cool enough to handle, lay it between 2 sheets of parchment paper on a baking sheet. Put another sheet on top to keep it flat and bake at 325°F until crisp, about 45 minutes. Break the skin into pieces and store in an airtight container.

SERVES 30

1 lb cured pork fat (lardo)

1 cooked pig's head (see page 48)

12 oz cooked pig's tongues (about 4)

2 oz duck fat

2 lb large onions, peeled and diced

3 cups pig's blood

generous pinch freshly grated nutmeg

generous pinch cinnamon

½ tsp ground piment d'Espelette (Espelette chile)

2 tsp salt, plus extra for seasoning

¾ cup heavy cream

1 tbsp *each* chopped tarragon, chervil, and flat-leaf parsley

2 free-range egg whites

¼ cup sherry vinegar

1 lb large pork sausage casings (optional – can use terrines)

all-purpose flour, for dusting

olive oil, for frying

CRISPY PORK SKIN

large piece of pork skin with 1/16 inch of fat

coarse sea salt

Jambon persillé

HAM TERRINE WITH PARSLEY

As a young chef I worked in a charcuterie in Paris and
this was one of my favorite terrines – both to make and
to eat. Very French, very easy, this is great for a party
and keeps well in the fridge for about ten days.

Cut the gammon into big chunks of about 4 inches and place them in a large
saucepan of cold water with the foot. Bring the water to a boil and cook for
3 minutes, then drain and rinse the meat.

Put back the gammon and foot back into the rinsed pan and add the wine,
peppercorns, and juniper berries. Tie the parsley, tarragon, and thyme
together and add them to the pan.

Add enough water to cover the meat. Slowly bring the liquid to a very, very
gentle simmer – barely a tremble – and continue to cook the meat until
tender, about 1½ hours. Skim often to remove any scum and excess fat.

Once the gammon is cooked, allow it to cool a little before removing it from
the pan and setting it aside to drain. Keep the cooking liquid.

Pass the cooking liquid through a square of cheesecloth. You should have
about 1⅔ cup, but if there is too much, bring it to a boil and reduce. Soak the
gelatin in a small bowl of cold water to soften, then remove and squeeze out
the excess liquid. Add the gelatin to the hot stock and stir well to melt.

Cut the gammon into small bite-sized cubes and place them in a bowl. Leave
some or all of the fat and skin, as it is delicious.

When the cooking liquid is semi-set and has the consistency of cream,
add the chopped parsley, tarragon vinegar, and nutmeg, season with black
pepper, and mix with the gammon. Pour all of this into a large glass bowl or
terrine, cover, and refrigerate overnight.

Turn the terrine out on to a plate to enjoy its full splendor, or spoon out
wedges to serve with plenty of toasted country-style bread and mustard.

SERVES 12

2 lb good-quality green
    gammon (uncooked
    country ham) leg meat, off
    the bone and preferably
    with some skin and fat
½ pig's foot, split
1⅓ cups dry white wine
6 whole black peppercorns
3 juniper berries
1 bunch of flat-leaf parsley
1 bunch of tarragon
1 sprig of thyme

JELLY

3 leaves of gelatin
1 bunch of flat-leaf parsley,
    chopped
1 tbsp tarragon vinegar
grating of nutmeg
toasted country-style bread
    and mustard, for serving
    (optional)
black pepper

Terrine de poireaux au fromage de chèvre

LEEK TERRINE WITH GOAT CHEESE

This is a very simple but effective vegetable terrine that makes a lovely light starter with the goat cheese cream suggested here. If you can't find goat curd, use a soft goat cheese and mash it with the crème fraîche – or simply serve with a beautiful goat cheese.

Bring a large pan of water to a boil and season with a generous amount of salt and a little sugar. Add the leeks and cook them until tender, 10–12 minutes. Check with the point of a knife – it should pierce the leeks easily. When the leeks are ready, carefully remove them from the pan and drain them on a rack so they keep their shape.

Line a terrine dish measuring about 9½ x 3 inches with a double layer of plastic wrap, leaving plenty of plastic wrap overlapping the sides. Place the whole leeks in the terrine, arranging them head to tail so you get alternating strips of green and white in the terrine. Wrap the overlapping plastic wrap tightly over the top and pierce it a few times with the point of a knife.

Now you need to weigh down the terrine to press out the excess water. The ideal way of doing this is to place another terrine of exactly the same size inside the first dish and weigh that down with heavy weights. Alternatively, place a small board inside the terrine, covering the leeks, and put a weight on top. It does need to be really heavy to press out the water. Place the whole thing on a tray to catch the water and leave in the fridge overnight.

The next day, to make the goat cheese cream, mash the goat curd with the crème fraîche until smooth and light, then season with salt, pepper, chopped chives, and a drizzle of olive oil.

Carefully turn the terrine out on to a serving dish and cut it into slices with a sharp knife. Serve with the goat cheese cream.

SERVES 12—14

salt
pinch sugar
20 medium leeks, trimmed, washed, and left whole

GOAT CHEESE CREAM

6 oz soft goat curd or goat cheese
8 oz crème fraîche
1 tbsp chopped chives
olive oil
salt
black pepper

Petit pâté de Pézenas

SWEET MUTTON PIES

These little sweet, spicy mutton pies were first
introduced to France by Clive of India, who ordered his
servants to cook them when he stayed near the village of
Pézenas in the Languedoc-Roussillon region. The pies
caught on and have become a classic dish. It is essential
to get the right balance of sweet, salty, and spicy flavors,
so check the seasoning carefully. The size and shape of a
spool of thread, the pies make a lovely starter for a special
meal, or could be served with salad as a light lunch.

Make the pastry first, as it needs to rest before use. Mix the flour and salt
in a bowl, then work in the butter with your fingertips. Add ½ cup water and
bring the pastry into a ball. Wrap it in plastic wrap and leave it in the fridge
to rest for 30 minutes.

Check that you've removed all the sinew and gristle from the lamb or mutton
and chop the meat with the kidney fat to make a coarse mixture. Season with
the spices, sugar, and salt and pepper and add the lemon zest. Quickly fry
a tiny piece of the mixture and taste it to make sure that you have the right
balance of flavors.

Roll out the pastry until it is quite thin and cut out 5 strips measuring
8 x 2½ inches, then cut 10 discs of 2½ inches across for the tops and bases.
Take a pastry disc, place it on a baking sheet, and arrange a strip on top,
shaping it round like a spool. Use a little beaten egg or water to seal the edge
in place. Repeat to make 4 more little pastry shells.

Preheat the oven to 425°F. Carefully fill each pastry shell with the meat
mixture and top with a pastry disc. Use a little beaten egg or water to stick
down the edges and then make a little incision on the top. Cook the pies
in the preheated oven until golden and cooked through, about 20 minutes.
Serve warm.

MAKES 5 PIES

PASTRY
2 cups all-purpose flour
2 pinches salt
6 tbsp cold unsalted butter,
    diced
beaten egg or water

FILLING
8 oz lamb or mutton
    shoulder, trimmed
4 oz lamb kidney fat
pinch *each* cumin and
    cinnamon
grating of nutmeg
½ tsp demerara sugar
grated zest of 1 lemon
salt
black pepper

Tête de porc et sa salade aux noisettes

PIG'S HEAD WITH HAZELNUT SALAD

This is a perfect example of something very delicious made with parts of an animal that some might think inedible. It's best served not too cold, so remember to take the dish out of the fridge for a while before serving.

Place the cleaned pig's head and cheeks in a large pan with the onion, celery, carrot, and herbs. Cover with cold water, add salt, and bring to a very gentle simmer. Continue to simmer until the meat is tender, 2 hours. Leave to cool in the liquid.

When the head is cool enough to handle, take it out of the pan, keeping the cooking liquid. Bring the cooking liquid to a boil again and cook until reduced. Carefully remove the bones from the head and lay one half, skin-side down, on a tray lined with plastic wrap. Pick the meat off the skin from both halves of the head and shred, then shred the cheek and tongue meat. Add the sliced ears, then season well with salt and pepper and moisten with a little of the reduced cooking liquor.

Spread this mixture on top of the skin and place the other half, skin-side up, on top. Cover with plastic wrap, place some weights on top, and leave in the fridge to set.

To make the garnish, roast the shallots in their skins at 400°F for 30 minutes. Discard the skins and purée the flesh in a food processor until smooth.

Whisk the honey, vinegar, and mustard with the oil to make the dressing, then season lightly with salt and pepper. Mix the leaves with the hazelnuts and apple sticks and drizzle with the dressing.

Cut the pig's head into slices and serve with the salad, shallot purée, and some bread or toasted baguette rubbed with a cut clove of garlic.

SERVES 10–12

1 pig's head, including tongue, split in half
4 pig cheeks
1 onion, peeled and roughly chopped
1 celery rib, roughly chopped
1 carrot, peeled and roughly chopped
2 bay leaves
1 sprig of thyme
salt
black pepper

GARNISH

4 shallots
½ tbsp clear honey
1 tbsp sherry vinegar
½ tbsp whole-grain mustard
4 tbsp hazelnut oil
mixed baby salad leaves
6 tbsp toasted hazelnuts, crushed
1 green apple, cut into matchsticks
salt
black pepper
bread, for serving
garlic clove, for rubbing

Caillettes de porc aux herbes

PORK LIVER PARCELS WITH HERBS

Every butcher and charcutier makes his own version of these delicious little meaty parcels, and I can't think of another dish that's found in so many parts of France. When you've nothing in the fridge, you can pop round the corner to buy some caillettes and serve them hot or cold for an instant snack or meal – they are so versatile. I like them cold with some hot toasted or grilled bread, drizzled with olive oil. Some recipes include some chard, spinach, or sorrel leaves in the mixture. If you want to add this, you need to cook the leaves gently in a little oil until tender, then drain them and squeeze out any excess water before adding them to the meat.

SERVES 4

7 oz pig's liver
9 oz pork fat
4 oz pork shoulder
2 garlic cloves, peeled and chopped
4 oz mixed herbs such as chives, sage, and parsley, chopped
2 shallots, peeled and chopped
6 oz pork caul fat
salt
black pepper

Mince the liver, pork fat, and shoulder, then mix in the garlic, herbs, and shallots. Season the mixture well. (If using chard, spinach, or sorrel, cook them as decribed above and add to the meat mixture at this stage.) Preheat the oven to 400°F.

Rinse the caul fat and lay it out on the work surface. Divide the meat into 4 or 5 balls and place them on the caul fat. Wrap the meatballs individually in the fat, tearing it as you go, and place them in an ovenproof dish – they should fit snugly. Bake in the preheated oven for 30 minutes.

Serve hot or cold, as a main dish or a snack.

Dans le cochon, tout est bon

Everything in a pig is good
GRIMOD DE LA REYNIÈRE

Foie gras rôti aux raisins

ROAST FOIE GRAS WITH RAISINS

A speciality of southwest France, foie gras is particularly good served with a local sweet wine such as Barsac or Sauternes. Be sure to keep the fat that is rendered as the liver cooks, and use it in another dish.

SERVES 4 AS A STARTER OR
2—3 AS A MAIN COURSE

30 seedless white grapes
⅓ cup golden raisins
¼ cup dry white wine
¼ cup marc de Bourgogne (or grappa)
1 whole duck foie gras (1 lb)
2 shallots, peeled and finely chopped
1 tbsp superfine sugar
2 tbsp sherry vinegar
¾ cup duck stock
salt
black pepper

To peel the grapes, plunge them into a pan of boiling water for a few seconds, then remove and refresh in iced water. Using a sharp knife, gently remove the skins and put the grapes in a bowl. Blanch the raisins in boiling water for 30 seconds, then drain and add them to the bowl with the grapes. Pour in the white wine and marc and leave the grapes and raisins to marinate for at least a couple of hours.

Preheat the oven to 425°F. Break the duck foie gras into 2 natural pieces and remove any obvious nerves, blemishes, or green stains from the gall bladder, which may be bitter. Season the liver well, place it in a cold ovenproof pan, and put it into the hot oven. Cook for 10 minutes, then turn the liver over and baste it with the rendered fat. Continue to cook until the smaller of the lobes of foie gras is firm to touch and cooked through; this should be no more than 15 minutes in total. Remove and let rest in a warm place while the larger lobe cooks for a further 10 minutes. Place it with the smaller one, drain off the fat into a bowl, and store in the fridge.

Using the same pan, sweat the shallots until translucent, then add the sugar and vinegar. Cook for a couple of minutes, then add the marinade from the grapes and raisins and boil until reduced to a glaze. Add the stock and reduce again until it has the consistency of a sauce. Pour this over the grapes and raisins and serve hot with the liver.

Rillettes de lapin

RABBIT RILLETTES

Rillettes can be made from many different meats but this recipe is one of my favorites. You can vary the seasoning if you like by adding ingredients such as green peppercorns or toasted pistachios. I like to serve these rillettes straight from a glass parfait jar, but if you are feeling in the mood for something fancy, shape them into neat quenelles with a tablespoon. Serve with hot toast and cornichons.

Cut the pork back fat into small cubes, put these in a large saucepan, and cover with plenty of water – about 2 quarts. Simmer for about an hour, until the fat has softened and become translucent, and the water has evaporated. Add the bouquet garni, onion, carrot, garlic, bacon, and ½ bottle of the white wine. Season generously with salt, pepper, and a grating of nutmeg – when cold, the rillettes will taste bland if not slightly overseasoned now.

Add the rabbit and diced pork to the pan and stir well. Cover with a piece of parchment paper and turn down the heat so the mixture is barely simmering. Cook for about 2 hours, stirring occasionally, until the meat is so soft that it crumbles.

Take the pan off the heat and pour the mixture into a clean bowl set over ice. Add ¾ cup more wine and stir vigorously with a spatula until cold. The rillette mixture will change color and turn opaque-white from the emulsified fat. Put the rillettes into jars or a terrine dish and store in the fridge. It will keep for 2–3 weeks.

15—20 SERVINGS

2½ lb pork back fat

bouquet garni, made up of celery, leek, 2 bay leaves, parsley stalks, and thyme (see page 342)

1 onion, peeled and studded with 2 cloves

1 carrot, peeled

3 garlic cloves, peeled

5 oz smoked bacon, diced

1 bottle dry white wine

freshly grated nutmeg

one 2½-lb rabbit (not wild), boned and cut up

1 lb pork shoulder, cut into large dice

salt

black pepper

Terrine de poisson

FISH TERRINE

This recipe does make a large terrine but it keeps for
a week in the fridge and can be served hot or cold.
The beautiful green color comes from the natural
chlorophyll in the green leaves – a trick I learned from
my father and not known to many chefs nowadays.

SERVES 14–16

1 lb fillets of white fish, such
as whiting, skinned and
pin bones removed
3 free-range egg whites
up to 3¼ cups heavy cream
unsalted butter, for greasing
7 oz large-leaf spinach, well
washed and stalks removed
1 bunch of watercress
1 bunch of curly-leaf parsley
6 large fillets of sole or plaice
10 oz fresh salmon
herb mayonnaise (see
page 333) or beurre blanc
(see page 332).
salt
black pepper

Blitz the 500 grams of white fish in a blender with the egg whites to make a
smooth purée. Pass this through a fine food mill into a bowl, making sure
you scrape all the mixture off the base of the mill. Place the bowl over ice
and gently beat in enough cream to make it the consistency of mayonnaise.
You may not need all the cream, so add it in stages. Season well, then test
the mousse for texture and taste. To do this, bring a small pan of seasoned
water to the simmering point and drop in a teaspoon of mousse. Cook for
3–4 minutes, then taste and add more cream or seasoning if necessary.

Butter a terrine measuring about 12 x 5 x 4 inches. Bring a pan of water
to a boil and add enough large spinach leaves to line the terrine. Drain
immediately and plunge the leaves into cold water, then use them to line the
terrine, leaving no gaps and letting them hang over the edge of the dish.

Blitz the remaining spinach with the watercress and parsley and enough
water to make a wet mulch. Press this against a fine strainer to extract all
the liquid. Put this liquid in a pan over medium heat, being careful not
to let it boil, or the chlorophyll will loose its vibrant color. Skim the solid
matter floating on the top and drain it on a piece of cheesecloth – this is
the chlorophyll.

Spoon half of the mousse into another bowl and add enough chlorophyll to
color it green. Pound the sole fillets to flatten them slightly and lay them in
a row on plastic wrap. Season, then spread some of the white mousse over
them. Lay a thick strip (¾–1¼ inches) of salmon over the mousse and roll it
all up. Add a layer of white mousse to the terrine, then add the white fish and
salmon roll. Finish with alternating layers of green and white mousse and
fold the spinach over the top. Cover with buttered foil.

Preheat the oven to 325°F. Put the terrine in a roasting pan, pour in boiling
water to come halfway up the sides, then bake for 1½ hours. Remove and let
cool completely before slicing. Serve cold with herb mayonnaise or warm
with beurre blanc. If serving warm, gently reheat the slices in a steamer.

*La cuisine c'est beaucoup
plus que des recettes*

Cooking is much more than recipes

ALAIN CHAPEL

Mousse de jambon

HAM MOUSSE

This really is a step back in time, when grand cuisine was all about mousses, jellies, and elaborate decorations. But with a light, delicate, modern touch, this classic recipe definitely deserves a comeback. The truffle is an extravagance but really does finish the dish.

To make the béchamel, bring the milk to a boil with the clove-studded onion, bay leaf, and salt and pepper. Cover and set aside. Gently melt the butter in a small pan and stir in the flour, then whisk and cook for 3–4 minutes over low heat. Strain the milk into the butter and flour, then whisk to get rid of any lumps. Bring the sauce to a boil, then turn down the heat and cook for 15 minutes. Dot with a little butter to avoid a skin foaming.

Trim any fat and sinew off the ham, then purée it in a food processor with ¾ cup of the béchamel sauce until smooth. Melt 1¼ cups of the jelly in a pan, setting the rest aside for later. Add the melted jelly to the mixture in the processor with the whipped cream, a grating of nutmeg, and salt and pepper. Process until smooth. For a super-fine mousse, press the mixture through a fine sieve before adding the jelly, cream, and seasoning.

Leave the mousse in the fridge overnight to set. When you're ready to serve, dip 2 soup spoons in hot water and shape the mousse into quenelles (neat egg shapes). Decorate them with slices of hard-boiled egg white and truffle and serve with the rest of the Madeira jelly and toasted brioche.

SERVES 8

BÉCHAMEL SAUCE

2 cups milk

1 white onion, peeled and studded with 2 cloves

1 bay leaf

3 tbsp unsalted butter, plus extra for dotting the surface

½ cup all-purpose flour

salt

black pepper

MOUSSE

12 oz best-quality cooked ham

1⅔ cup Madeira jelly (see page 336)

¾ cup heavy cream, whipped

freshly grated nutmeg

salt

black pepper

GARNISH

whites of 2 hard-boiled free-range eggs, sliced

1 truffle, sliced

toasted brioche

Pâté de volaille et pistaches

CHICKEN AND PORK PÂTÉ WITH PISTACHIOS

This is what we call a *pâté grandmère*. It's a traditional country-style pâté and a great staple to have in the fridge for everyone to help themselves to whenever they want. In France there are 101 varieties of pâté and terrines, which can be made in anything from cake tins to parfait jars. I'm never without them. You can make this recipe with any poultry you like and use hazelnuts instead of pistachios if you prefer. Serve with pickled onions or gherkins, toast, and salad leaves.

Cut each of the chicken breasts lengthwise into 3 big slices and set them aside. Mix the chicken livers into the minced pork and season, then add the lemon zest, shallots, thyme, and pistachios.

Line a mold, such as an 8-inch cake pan or earthenware dish, with overlapping strips of bacon, making sure it is completely covered and leaving some bacon hanging over the edges. Press in half the pork mixture, add the chicken pieces, then cover with the rest of the pork. Fold the bacon stips over to encase the filling.

Preheat the oven to 400°F. Place the dish in a roasting pan and pour in enough boiling water to come about halfway up the sides. Bake for 45 minutes–1 hour, depending on the size of the mold. Check that the pâté is done by piercing the center with a needle. The juices should run clear and the needle should feel hot to the touch.

Allow to cool, then chill overnight in the fridge. Turn out and serve in slices.

SERVES 8

3 boneless, skinless free-range chicken half-breasts
4 oz free-range chicken livers, trimmed
6 oz pork belly (fatty), minced
1½ tsp salt
2 tsp ground black pepper
grated zest of 1 unwaxed lemon
2 shallots, peeled and finely chopped
2 sprigs of lemon thyme, chopped
6 tbsp shelled pistachios (blanched)
20–25 thin strips bacon, depending on the size of your mold

Cou de canard farci

STUFFED DUCK NECK

This is a traditional way of using duck necks in southwest France and is usually served cold with a little salad or some radishes. Alternatively, Cumberland sauce, that great British accompaniment for cold cuts, also goes well.

The duck necks should be as long as possible and have no holes. Remove the neck bones, sinew, and excess fat. Using butcher's string, tie off each neck at the thin end to ready it for stuffing.

Chop the meat, fat, and foie gras into ⅜-inch dice. Mince a third of this as finely as possible, then fold it into the rest of the meat. Add the thyme leaves, pistachios, and truffle and season with the coriander and salt and pepper. Pour the duck stock into a small pan and reduce it to a sticky syrup, then fold it into the mixture.

Push the stuffing into the necks, making sure there are no air pockets, and tie the ends securely with butcher's string. Take a pan that's big enough for the duck necks to lie flat and add water and a pinch of salt. Heat the water to 160°F, then add the duck necks and poach them gently for 40 minutes.

Take the pan off the heat and leave the necks to cool a little, then remove them and refrigerate. They are best left to mature for 48 hours before slicing and serving, and they keep well for a couple of weeks in the fridge.

SERVES 10 AS A STARTER

2 duck necks
1 lb duck meat, cleaned
    of fat and sinew
4 oz pork back fat
12 oz cooked foie gras
2 tsp chopped thyme leaves
½ cup pistachios (shelled
    weight), chopped
6 tbsp cooked truffle,
    chopped
pinch ground coriander
1 cup duck stock
    (see page 322)
salt
black pepper

Cheese and eggs make a wonderful marriage, but cheese on its own is truly delicious. No meal in France, however casual, is complete without a little cheese. For me, eggs are the simplest and most satisfying of fast food. They are so versatile, used in everything from the quickest snack to the most elaborate recipes. And eggs are not just an ingredient in French cooking – they can be the focal point of many recipes and have inspired some great classics. There's nothing as French as a perfect omelette.

Oeufs et fromage

Croque monsieur

TOASTED HAM AND CHEESE SANDWICH

Properly made with béchamel sauce, this classic
French hot sandwich is a delight – but it is all too easy
to find disappointing versions. Try preparing your
own to enjoy the croque in its full glory.

Lightly toast the bread on both sides, then butter one side of each slice.

To make the béchamel sauce, melt the remaining butter in a small pan,
stir in the flour to make a roux, then whisk in the milk. Keep whisking it
well to avoid lumps and bring the sauce to a boil. Season with salt, pepper,
and nutmeg and cook for 3–4 minutes, then remove from the heat.

Preheat the oven to 400°F. Spread a little mustard on the buttered side of
a piece of toast. Add a generous amount of béchamel, followed by grated
cheese and a slice of ham. Spread some more béchamel on the dry side of
another piece of toast and place on top of the ham, pressing a little to stick
it down. Spread a little more béchamel on top of the sandwich and sprinkle
with grated cheese. Make all the sandwiches in the same way.

Put the sandwiches on a baking sheet and bake them in the preheated oven
until crisp and golden, 6–8 minutes. Serve at once.

SERVES 4

8 slices good sourdough
    bread
2 tbsp unsalted butter
1 tbsp all-purpose flour
1⅔ cup milk
freshly grated nutmeg
Dijon mustard
2 cups grated cheese
    (a mixture of Emmental,
    Gruyère, and Cheddar
    is good)
5 oz sliced good-quality ham
salt
black pepper

Tartiflette

CHEESE AND POTATO BAKE

A classic from the Haute-Savoie region in the French Alps, tartiflette is a hearty dish that has become a favorite on bistro menus. It's simple to prepare and makes a good lunch on a cold winter's day.

SERVES 6

2 lb red-skinned potatoes
8 oz ventrèche (see page 343) or pancetta
vegetable oil
1 lb Reblochon cheese, chopped
salt
black pepper

Peel the potatoes and cut them into large dice. Wash in cold water, then put them in a pan of salted water and bring to a boil. Cook for 3 minutes, then drain well.

Cut the ventrèche into lardons and put them in a large frying pan over medium heat with a dash of vegetable oil. Gently fry the lardons until the fat starts running, then add the potatoes. Continue to cook for 5–6 minutes, stirring occasionally and scraping the pan if necessary, until the potatoes have taken on a little color. Preheat the oven to 425°F.

Season the potatoes and tip everything into an ovenproof dish. Scatter the chopped cheese on top and bake in the hot oven for 15 minutes. Finish under a preheated grill to brown the top.

Oeufs brouillés Alexandra

SCRAMBLED EGGS WITH CHOUX BUNS AND CHICKEN

I love scrambled eggs – the creamier the better – and
I'll eat them at any time of day, as a starter or a main
meal. I first came across this rather special version when
working at the Élysée Palace for President Mitterrand.

First make the choux buns. Preheat the oven to 475°F. Pour ½ cup water
and the milk into a pan, add the butter, salt, and sugar and bring to a boil.
Take the pan off the heat and beat in the flour. Once all the flour has been
incorporated, put the pan back on the heat and cook for 6–7 minutes,
stirring continuously. Take the pan off the heat again and beat in 4 of the
eggs, one at a time, and mix until smooth. The mixture might look as though
it is separating, but keep beating and it will all come together.

Put the mixture into a piping bag and pipe 24 little rounds onto a nonstick
baking sheet, taking care to keep them all about the same size and shape so
they cook evenly. Beat the remaining egg and use it to brush the buns, then
bake them for 5 minutes. Open the oven door to release the steam, turn the
temperature down to 400°F, and cook until crisp and cooked, another
12–15 minutes. Remove and place on a rack to cool.

Season the chicken breasts with salt and pepper. Heat the butter in a frying
pan until foaming and fry the chicken until golden on both sides and very
pink inside. Take the chicken out of the pan and discard the butter. Deglaze
the pan with the port, then cook to reduce by half. Add the chicken jus and
reduce to a sauce consistency. Cut the chicken into small dice, put it back
in the sauce, and continue to cook until done.

Now for the eggs. Use all the butter to grease a heavy-bottomed saucepan,
then add the beaten eggs and cook over medium heat while stirring with
a spatula. When the eggs are almost completely cooked, season and pour
in the heavy cream.

To serve, cut the tops off the choux buns and fill them three-quarters full
with scrambled eggs, followed by the chicken mixture. Place the lids back
on top and serve immediately.

SERVES 8 AS A STARTER

CHOUX BUNS (MAKES 24)
½ cup milk
6 tbsp unsalted butter
1 pinch salt
2 pinches sugar
1¼ cups all-purpose flour
5 free-range eggs

CHICKEN
2 free-range chicken half-
    breasts, skinned
1 tbsp unsalted butter
2 tbsp port
¾ cup chicken jus
    (see page 328)
salt
black pepper

EGGS
2 tbsp unsalted butter
16 free-range eggs, beaten
6 tbsp heavy cream
salt
black pepper

Oeufs friands

SCRAMBLED EGGS WITH WOODCOCK

This was originally eaten as a savory at the end of a meal, but I like to serve it as a starter or lunch dish or even as a light main course. Traditionally this recipe was served in puff pastry *vol-au-vents,* but I prefer the toasted brioche, which adds a little richness and texture to this extravagant, luxurious delight.

Prepare the woodcocks for roasting and remove the guts — or ask your butcher to do this for you. Set the upper intestines, heart, and liver aside for later, but discard the gizzard, which will be full of gravel. Season the woodcocks and push the beak through the legs to hold it in place.

Preheat the oven to 425°F. Heat the oil in a roasting pan on top of the stove, add the woodcocks, and brown them briefly. Add a tablespoon of the butter and heat until it is foaming but not burnt, then put the pan of woodcocks in the hot oven for no more than 8 minutes — the meat should still be very pink. Let rest in a warm place.

Drain the fat from the roasting pan and discard, then add another tablespoon of butter to the pan and heat it on the stove top. When the butter is hot, add the chopped shallot and garlic, cook for 30 seconds, then add the woodcock entrails and chicken livers. Season well and cook over high heat just until cooked pink, 2 minutes, then add the brandy and flambé. Press the mixture through a fine sieve, then spread it over the toasted brioche and keep warm. Remove the breasts from the woodcocks and split each head in half along the beak.

Grease a heavy-bottomed pan with the remaining butter, then add the eggs and cook over medium heat while stirring with a spatula. When the eggs are almost completely cooked, season and add the heavy cream. Keep them nice and creamy — don't overcook them. Serve the eggs with the brioche, a woodcock breast, and half a head. Add a little game jus, if you like.

SERVES 4

2 woodcocks
1 tbsp vegetable oil
3 tbsp unsalted butter
1 shallot, peeled and finely chopped
½ garlic clove, peeled and finely chopped
2 free-range chicken livers
1 tbsp brandy
4 thick slices of brioche lightly toasted and crusts removed
8 free-range eggs, beaten
2 tbsp heavy cream
game jus (optional — see page 329)
salt
black pepper

Omelette aux girolles

OMELETTE WITH CHANTERELLES

Omelettes are an essential in the French kitchen, and everyone has a favorite version. During the wild mushroom season a *poêlée* of chanterelles with just a hint of new season garlic and parsley makes the humble omelette into a feast fit for a prince. Then comes the truffle season, and a truffle omelette is food for a king. Another of my favorites is with grated goat cheese, especially the Pélardon cheese from the Cévennes. It's so dry that it is impossible to bite into, but when grated into a perfectly *baveuse* omelette it's heavenly.

SERVES 2

4 free-range eggs (or 6 if greedy)

4 oz chanterelle mushrooms or any wild mushrooms, such as morels or porcini

vegetable oil

½ garlic clove, peeled and finely chopped

1 tbsp finely chopped flat-leaf parsley

2 tbsp unsalted butter

salt

black pepper

Crack the eggs into a bowl, beat them with a fork, and season with salt and pepper. Trim and wipe the mushrooms, then fry them in a little oil and add the finely chopped garlic and parsley. Season and set aside.

Heat an 8-inch omelette pan until it's very hot, then add a drop of oil and the butter. Wait till the butter is golden, but don't let it burn. Pour in the eggs and leave the pan for 20 seconds or so before starting to mix them with a fork or spatula. Once the omelette has formed and is holding but still a little underdone, add the mushrooms in the center and carefully roll the omelette over them to the edge of the pan.

Flip the omelette on to a warm plate and cut it in half to serve. It should have a little color but be light and fluffy – brush with a little butter to give it a lovely shine and gloss.

Soufflé aux épinards

SPINACH SOUFFLÉ

A soufflé is an impressive dish, but not hard to do once you've mastered the technique. You'll need 4 ramekins measuring 3 by 2½ inches if making individual soufflés, or one 8-inch dish. The béchamel sauce recipe makes more than you need for the soufflé, but it keeps in the fridge for a week. Cover it well, though.

If you'd like to serve the soufflé with a sauce such as tomato coulis, prepare that first and hold it at the ready.

Bring a pan of salted water to a boil and blanch the spinach for 30 seconds. Plunge it into iced water to refresh, then drain and press out some of the water with your hands. Blitz the spinach in a food processor until smooth, then place it in a clean cloth and press and squeeze out as much water as you can until the spinach purée is as dry as possible.

To make the béchamel, melt the butter in a small pan. Stir in the flour and cook for 3–4 minutes without letting it color, then whisk in the milk. Bring to a boil and whisk until the sauce is smooth. Season with a grating of nutmeg and some salt and pepper, then cover to avoid a skin forming.

Preheat the oven to 400°F. Butter your ramekins or mold and coat the insides with grated Parmesan. Put 4 tablespoons of béchamel in a bowl, add 4 tablespoons of the spinach, and mix well with the 2 egg yolks. Whisk the egg whites in a separate bowl with a pinch of salt until stiff, then fold into the béchamel and spinach mixture until smooth. Do not overmix.

Pour the mixture into the ramekins or mold and level off the top with a spatula. Run a knife or your thumb around the inside rim to ensure a straight rise. Place in the preheated oven and cook for 8–10 minutes for individual souffles or 16–18 minutes for the bigger one. Serve immediately on its own or with a sauce such as tomato coulis.

SERVES 4

tomato coulis (optional – see page 336)

14 oz leaf spinach

BÉCHAMEL SAUCE

2½ tbsp unsalted butter

⅓ cup all-purpose flour

¾ cup milk

freshly grated nutmeg

salt

black pepper

unsalted butter, for greasing

2 oz Parmesan cheese, grated

2 medium free-range egg yolks

8 medium free-range egg whites

pinch salt

Surtout, faites simple

Above all, keep it simple

AUGUSTE ESCOFFIER

Poireaux vinaigrette aux oeufs

LEEK SALAD EGG VINAIGRETTE

Make this simple French classic with young, tender leeks for a perfect lunch or starter.

Trim off the dark green tops of the leeks, leaving about 1¼ inches of the light green. Bring a large pan of salted water to a boil, add the leeks, and cook until tender – this should take about 6 minutes. Drain the leeks and lay them flat on a rack to cool slightly while you make the vinaigrette.

Put the mustard, vinegar, and seasoning in a bowl with a little of the water. Whisk as if making a mayonnaise, slowly adding the oil to emulsify the vinaigrette. Add a little more water if the mixture becomes too thick.

Cut the leeks in half lengthwise and arrange them on a dish or plate. Scatter the chopped egg and snipped chives over. Drizzle with the vinaigrette and eat while the leeks are still warm.

SERVES 4

16 young leeks, washed
2 free-range eggs, hard-
   boiled and chopped
1 bunch of chives, snipped
salt
black pepper

VINAIGRETTE
2 tbsp Dijon mustard
2 tbsp red wine vinegar
4–6 tbsp water
1¼ cups vegetable or
   peanut oil

Oeufs pochés à la Rossini

POACHED EGGS WITH TRUFFLE AND MADEIRA SAUCE

Sheer extravagance, this recipe is as old as the more well-known *tournedos Rossini.* Both were created by Antonin Carême, one of the most famous nineteenth-century French chefs, in honor of the Italian composer Rossini, who famously loved his food. Both are rich, luxurious dishes fit for a special occasion.

First make the sauce. Put the shallots in a saucepan with the sliced mushrooms and a little of the butter and cook over medium heat until the shallots are caramelized. Add the port and Madeira, bring to a boil, and cook until reduced by half. Add the stock and truffle juice and simmer syrupy, skimming regularly, about 20 minutes.

Remove the pan from the heat and pass the sauce through a fine sieve, pressing well to extract as much flavor as possible. Cut the remaining butter into cubes. Pour the sauce back into the pan, bring it to a boil, and add the cubes of cold butter to thicken the sauce and give it a luster. Season with salt and pepper and a few drops of vinegar to balance the sweetness, then set aside and keep warm.

Cut the brioche into 3-inch rounds and trim the slices of foie gras terrine to fit – devour the trimmings as you do this. Warm the clarified butter in a pan and lightly fry the brioche slices. Drain and set aside.

Bring a pan of water to a boil and add the vinegar. This helps to set the white part of the egg so that it has an elegant shape – salting the water has the opposite effect. Crack the eggs into separate bowls. Swirl the water with a spoon, gently add the eggs, and poach until cooked but with soft yolks, 5 minutes. Carefully remove the eggs with a slotted spoon.

While the eggs are cooking, place a slice of foie gras on each piece of brioche. If necessary, you could warm these briefly in the oven at 350°F. Trim the eggs neatly and place them on top of the foie gras. Decorate with thin slices of truffle and serve with the sauce.

If you'd like to get everything ready in advance to put together at the last minute, poach the eggs, then refresh them in iced water and set aside. When you're ready to serve, reheat the eggs for 30 seconds in a steamer over a pan of simmering water.

SERVES 4

4 thin slices of brioche
4 slices of cooked foie gras
2 tbsp clarified butter
    (see page 330)
1 tbsp white wine vinegar
4 duck eggs
2 oz black truffle

SAUCE

2 shallots, peeled and sliced
6 button mushrooms,
    wiped and sliced
2 tbsp cold unsalted butter
½ cup port
½ cup Madeira wine
2 cups veal stock
    (see page 322)
2 tbsp truffle juice
    (available in cans)
sherry vinegar
salt
black pepper

Oeufs cocotte au maïs et chorizo

BAKED EGGS WITH CORN AND CHORIZO

Eggs cooked in little pots – *en cocotte* – like this are
a popular classic in France and simple and quick to
prepare. This version makes a lovely starter or light
meal at any time.

Preheat the oven to 400°F. Take 4 small ovenproof dishes, such as
ramekins, and lightly butter the insides.

Pour a tablespoon of cream into each dish, followed by some drained
sweetcorn and a few slices of chorizo. Then carefully crack an egg into
each dish, lightly season with salt and pepper, and then cover with more
cream so the yolk can only just be seen. Season again, then place the dishes
in a roasting pan and pour in enough boiling water to come halfway up the
sides. Bake in the preheated oven until the egg whites have set but the yolks
are still runny, 6 minutes.

Sprinkle the eggs with a little paprika and serve immediately with some
toast strips.

SERVES 4

unsalted butter, for greasing
1½ cups heavy cream
¾ cup fresh corn kernels
2 oz Spanish-style firm
    chorizo, sliced
4 free-range eggs
paprika
toast strips, for serving
salt
black pepper

Oeufs pochés meurette

POACHED EGGS IN A RED WINE SAUCE

This Burgundian dish was another recipe I first encountered when I was working at the Élysée Palace in Paris during my military service. It was President Mitterrand's favorite – he liked it for breakfast. You need a good strong red wine, preferably from Burgundy, of course.

Crack the eggs into separate cups. Bring the red wine to a boil in a large pan. Stir to get the wine swirling, then carefully slip in the eggs and poach them until cooked but with soft yolks, 4 minutes. Remove the eggs with a slotted spoon and place them in iced water to refresh, then set aside until later. Keep the wine for the sauce.

Preheat the oven to 400°F. Cut 4 thin slices from the bacon, place them on a baking sheet, and cover with another baking sheet. Cook in the preheated oven until crisp. Put the rest of the bacon in a pan of cold water, bring to a boil, and simmer for 10 minutes, then cut into small lardons and set aside.

Pour 1 cup of the red wine into a pan and boil to reduce to a sticky glaze. Then add the stock and reduce again until it has the consistency of a sauce. Season with salt, pepper, and a pinch of sugar if necessary, then add a little of the butter to add shine to the sauce.

Melt a knob of butter in a frying pan, add the onions, and cook them until tender. Add a little of the sauce to glaze.

Sweat the chopped shallots and mushrooms in butter over low heat until tender, then season with salt and pepper. Add the cream and continue to cook until the mixture is thick. Pan-fry the bacon lardons until golden.

Cut the brioche into 2-inch circles and fry in the clarified butter until golden but not dry. Drain and set aside.

Now, put everything together. Gently reheat the eggs in a steamer over simmering water until warm but not overcooked, about 3 minutes. Place each egg on a slice of brioche on warm plates. Add neat spoonfuls of the mushroom mixture, lardons, onions, and crispy bacon, then spoon on some sauce. Serve immediately.

SERVES 4

4 free-range eggs
1 bottle of strong red wine
7 oz smoked bacon
   (in one piece)
1¼ cups veal stock
   (see page 322)
pinch sugar
½ cup unsalted butter
12 pearl onions, peeled
2 shallots, peeled and finely
   chopped
8 oz button mushrooms,
   wiped and finely chopped
¼ cup heavy cream
2 tbsp clarified butter
   (see page 330)
4 thick slices brioche
salt
black pepper

Oeufs pochés Carême

POACHED EGGS WITH SALMON AND ARTICHOKE HEARTS

Another classic created by Carême, this time for the French royal family. For an even more luxurious dish, top each one with a slice or two of truffle.

Peel off the leaves from each artichoke to reveal the heart. Trim to make the hearts a perfect round shape and remove the chokes with a teaspoon (see page 342). Bring a pan of salted water to a boil, add the artichoke hearts with a little vinegar to keep them from discoloring, and cook until they are tender, about 15 minutes. Remove and set aside.

Crack the eggs into separate bowls. Bring a pan of water with a dash of vinegar to a rolling boil, then swirl the water with a spoon, gently add the eggs, and poach them for 3–4 minutes. Refresh the eggs in iced water, then drain and trim.

For the mayonnaise, beat the egg in a bowl with the lemon juice and mustard until smooth. Slowly add the vegetable oil in a thin, steady stream, whisking continuously. Stir in the cream, Tabasco, and brandy.

Cut 2 circles of smoked salmon about the same size as the poached eggs. Chop the rest and add it to the mayonnaise with the chopped chives. Season with salt and pepper.

Fill the artichoke hearts with the salmon and mayonnaise mixture. Top each with a poached egg and a circle of smoked salmon, then serve at once.

SERVES 2

2 globe artichokes
white wine vinegar
2 free-range eggs
8 slices smoked salmon
1 bunch chives, chopped
salt
black pepper

MAYONNAISE
1 free-range egg
juice of ½ lemon
2 tsp Dijon mustard
6 tbsp vegetable oil
1 tbsp cream
1 tsp Tabasco sauce
1 tsp brandy

I love to cook and eat fish and enjoy everything from the very simplest dishes to more elaborate recipes. I grew up eating fish on Fridays, and this Catholic tradition still prevails in much of rural France. Even if you're not religious, this is an excellent custom to keep up — and healthy too. Good-quality fish is available all over France, often in local markets. In central France they probably eat more freshwater species, while in Brittany and Normandy shellfish are the stars of many recipes. Salt cod is particularly popular in southern France. Good farmed fish, such as salmon, bream, bass, turbot, and trout, is also available now at reasonable prices.

Poissons et fruits de mer

Huîtres Kilpatrick et huîtres Rockefeller

OYSTERS KILPATRICK AND OYSTERS ROCKEFELLER

Oysters are usually served raw in France, but sometimes I like to make these two wonderful recipes for cooked oysters. Kilpatrick is actually an Australian favorite, and the shellfish are partnered with bacon and bread crumbs. Oysters Rockefeller are named after the American billionaire, John D. Rockefeller, because the creamy sauce is so rich!

Shuck all the oysters, collecting all the juice, and clean the bottom shells.

For oysters Kilpatrick, pour the oyster juice into a wide pan. Add the oysters, bring to a simmer and cook for just a moment or two. Remove them and set aside, keeping the poaching liquor. Fry the bacon, then stir it into the bread crumbs and set aside a quarter of the mixture for sprinkling on top of the oysters. Mix the rest of the bacon and crumbs with the Worcestershire and Tabasco sauces to taste, the lemon juice and enough of the poaching liquor to make a thick sauce.

Divide this between the bottom shells and place the oysters on top. Sprinkle with the reserved bacon and bread crumb mixture and finish cooking under a hot broiler to brown and crisp the tops. Serve at once.

For oysters Rockefeller, blanch the spinach briefly in boiling water, then refresh in cold water. Drain the spinach well, then squeeze out as much water as possible and chop. Sweat the shallot in the butter, add the spinach, chopped parsley and a dash of cream to moisten, then season with grated nutmeg and pepper. Pour the oyster juice into a wide pan. Add the oysters, bring to a simmer and cook for a moment or two, then remove them and set aside, leaving the juices in the pan. Add a little pastis to the pan and reduce, then add the rest of cream and reduce again until the mixture is thick and creamy with the consistency of a sauce. Whisk in the egg yolk.

Place a little of the spinach mix into each bottom shell and top with an oyster, then some sauce. Put the oysters under a preheated broiler to bake and glaze or into a preheated oven at 425°F for a few minutes. Serve the oysters hot on a bed of rock salt and seaweed.

SERVES 2

KILPATRICK

6 medium rock oysters
2 oz smoked bacon, finely diced
1 cup fresh bread crumbs
Worcestershire sauce
Tabasco sauce
juice of ½ lemon

ROCKEFELLER

6 medium rock oysters
4 oz spinach
1 shallot, peeled and chopped
½ tbsp unsalted butter
1 tbsp chopped flat-leaf parsley
6 tbsp heavy cream
freshly grated nutmeg
2 tsp pastis
1 free-range egg yolk
rock salt and seaweed, for serving
black pepper

Salade chaude de coques, palourdes et pommes de terre

WARM COCKLE, CLAM AND POTATO SALAD

In France we use a good red wine vinegar for this salad but malt vinegar, British seaside style, can also work well – in fact, I love it. The salad is a traditional dish from the tiny island of Noirmoutier, off the coast of the Vendée, where they grow a superb range of early potatoes. The crops are fertilized with seaweed, giving them a beautifully salty flavor.

SERVES 4

2 lb cockles
2 lb Venus or cherrystone clams
2 shallots, 1 sliced, 1 finely chopped
1 cup dry white wine
8 oz marble-sized potatoes, a mix of colors if you can find them
1 tbsp good red wine vinegar
4 tbsp olive oil
1 bunch of flat-leaf parsley, finely chopped
ground piment d'Espelette (chile powder)
salt

Wash the cockles and clams well in cold water. Tip them into a very hot saucepan with the sliced shallot and the white wine. Cover and steam for 6–7 minutes until the shellfish have opened and are cooked. Drain and collect the cooking liquor. Discard any shellfish that do not open.

Pour the liquor into a small pan, bring it to a boil and reduce by half. Strain the reduced liquid through a fine sieve and keep it warm.

Pick the meat from the cockles and clams, saving a few clam shells for decoration. Boil the potatoes in salted water until tender. Peel them or not, as you prefer, and toss them while still warm with the cockles, clams, vinegar, oil and cooking liquor. Add the parsley and the finely chopped shallot, and sprinkle with a little piment d'Espelette before serving.

Dis-moi ce que tu manges, je te dirai qui tu es

Tell me what you eat, and I will tell you who you are

JEAN ANTHELME BRILLAT-SAVARIN

Ravioles de homard et St Jacques

PANFRIED LOBSTER AND SCALLOP RAVIOLI

This is my take on dim sum and uses a different sort of pasta dough from the normal kind. You can make the ravioli any shape you like, but they must contain the filling effectively and be well sealed, as they are fried briefly before serving.

First make the pasta dough. Put the flour in a bowl, add the remaining ingredients, and knead to make an elastic, but not sticky, dough. Leave the dough to rest in the fridge for at least 20 minutes, then roll it out on the 'o' setting on a pasta machine.

Chop the scallops into ⅛-inch dice. Break up the lobster, cutting the tail into quarters for the garnish. Extract all the rest of the lobster meat and cut into ¼-inch dice, then mix with the diced scallops and season with salt and a generous amount of pepper.

The shape of the ravioli is up to you, but the simplest method is to cut the pasta dough into 24 rounds about 2½ inches in diameter. Divide the scallop and lobster filling among 12 of the rounds. Brush the borders with water to moisten, then top with the remaining rounds and press down well around the edges to seal.

Bring a pan of salted water to a boil, add the ravioli, and cook for 4 minutes. Remove the ravioli and plunge them into iced water to stop the cooking, then carefully drain and dry on a cloth and lightly drizzle them with olive oil. Keep the ravioli refrigerated until needed.

For the sauce, put the shallots, garlic, and marjoram in a pan with the white wine and boil until the liquid has almost completely evaporated. Add the sun-dried tomatoes and lobster stock, then bring to a boil and simmer for 20 minutes. Pass the sauce through a fine sieve, then pour it back into the pan, season, and finish with the cold butter to thicken and shine. Keep the sauce warm while you finish the ravioli.

Pan-fry the ravioli in a hot nonstick pan until golden on both sides and hot inside. Serve in warm bowls with the piping hot sauce and garnish with diced tomatoes and lobster claws and a few marjoram leaves.

SERVES 4

PASTA DOUGH

2 cups all-purpose flour

⅓ cup free-range egg whites

3 tbsp warm water

1 tbsp olive oil

pinch salt

FILLING

8 large scallops
(white meat only)

1 lb cooked lobster

olive oil

salt

black pepper

SAUCE

2 shallots, peeled and sliced

1 garlic clove, peeled and
chopped

2 sprigs of marjoram

½ cup dry white wine

6 dry sun-dried tomatoes
(not in oil), chopped

2 cups lobster stock
(see page 325)

2 tbsp cold unsalted butter,
cubed

salt

black pepper

GARNISH

4 tomatoes, peeled, seeded,
and diced

marjoram leaves

Gratin de langoustines et escargots au piment d'Espelette

GRATIN OF LANGOUSTINES AND SNAILS WITH ESPELETTE CHILE

This has long been a favorite on the menu at Le Gavroche and it's a French classic that we now make with British snails. There's quite a bit of work involved, as you need to make a hollandaise to enrich the creamy sauce, but it's well worth the effort.

SERVES 8

HOLLANDAISE SAUCE
1 tbsp white wine vinegar
3 tbsp white wine
2 tbsp water
4 free-range egg yolks
1 cup butter, clarified
    (see page 330)
salt

4 bunches curly parsley,
    picked and washed
1²/₃ cup heavy cream
24 cooked langoustines
3 large shallots, peeled
1 cup dry white wine
1¼ cups fish stock
    (see page 324)
½ tbsp ground piment
    d'Espelette (chile powder)
2 tsp unsalted butter
24 cooked snails (canned or
    vacuum packed are fine)
2 garlic cloves, peeled and
    chopped
salt
black pepper

First make the hollandaise. Put the vinegar, wine, and water into a heavy-bottomed pan and bring to a boil. Add a pinch of salt, remove the pan from the heat, and let cool. Whisk in the egg yolks, then place the pan over very gentle heat and keep whisking, making sure the whisk comes into contact with the whole base of the pan. After 8–10 minutes the yolks will have emulsified and you can increase the heat a little. The mixture should not exceed 154°F – if too hot the yolks will scramble – and should become smooth and thick enough to form peaks. Take the pan off the heat and whisk in the clarified butter, then cover and keep the sauce in a warm place for later.

Bring a pan of salted water to a boil and blanch the parsley for 4–5 minutes. Drain, keeping the water, then refresh the parsley in iced water. Drain it again well, pressing to extract excess water. Heat 6 tablespoons of the cream to a boil. Put the parsley in a blender with a pinch of salt and the hot cream, then blitz until smooth, adding a little cooking water if needed.

Shell the langoustines and slice 2 of the shallots. Put the shallots in a pan with the wine and 6 of the langoustine heads, breaking them up with a spatula, then add a little salt and boil until the pan is almost dry. Add the stock and boil again until reduced by half, then add the rest of cream. Once the mixture has the consistency of a sauce, pass it through a fine sieve, then stir in the hollandaise and season with a little of the Espelette chile powder. Set aside.

Chop the remaining shallot. Warm a teaspoon of the butter in a pan and add the snails with the shallot and garlic. Warm through, making sure you don't burn the garlic, then remove the snails and set them aside. Add the rest of the butter to the pan and heat until foaming. Toss the langoustines in the Espelette chile powder, then add them to the pan to warm through. Preheat the broiler. Take 8 heatproof bowls and add 3 snails, 3 langoustines, and a little parsley purée to each one. Cover with the sauce, then place the bowls under the hot broiler to glaze. Serve immediately.

Fricassée de homard au citron et noix de coco

LOBSTER WITH LEMONGRASS AND COCONUT BISQUE

Although this might not sound like a French dish, it employs classic French techniques and has become an indulgent favorite at Le Gavroche over the years. We like to present it in the rather spectacular fashion shown in the photograph opposite, but if you prefer, simply serve the pieces of lobster on the lemon purée and pour in the warm bisque. I sometimes like to serve this with some seaweed pasta as well (see page 339).

First make the lemon purée. Bring the sugar and 5 tablespoons water to a boil to make a stock syrup, and set it aside. Put the lemons in a pan of cold water, bring to a boil, then drain. Repeat 10 times, adding fresh water each time, then set them aside until cool enough to handle. Cut the lemons open and remove any seeds, then place them in a blender – skins and all – and purée until smooth, adding some of the stock syrup to taste and a little salt. The purée should be sharp, so be careful not to add too much syrup. The purée sets when it is cool and keeps well for several weeks.

Bring a huge pan of salted water to a boil, add the lobsters, and cook them for 4 minutes. Remove them from the pan and let cool. Once the lobsters are cool enough to handle, take off their heads and set them aside. Crack the bodies and claws, remove the flesh, and cut into into bite-sized pieces. Keep the tails and tips of heads for garnishing the dish.

To make the bisque, put the remains of the lobsters (not the heads) in a pan with any juices and a little olive oil. Add the chopped shallots, carrot, celery, garlic, piment d'Espelette, and lemongrass. Cook gently for 6–7 minutes, then add the brandy and stir to deglaze the pan, followed by the white wine and the mirin. Continue to cook until the liquid has almost evaporated, then add the fish stock and tomato paste. Simmer for 20 minutes, then pass through a fine sieve. Tip the soup back into the pan and boil to reduce the liquid by half, then stir in the coconut cream and heavy cream.

Gently reheat the lobster meat in the melted butter and check the seasoning. Serve the lobster on a bed of lemon purée with white asparagus or salsify and slivers of fresh coconut, then pour in the warm bisque.

SERVES 4

LEMON PURÉE
6 tbsp sugar
5 unwaxed lemons (as fresh as possible)
salt

1 lb uncooked lobsters
2 tbsp olive oil
2 shallots, peeled and chopped
1 carrot, peeled and chopped
1 celery rib, chopped
1 garlic clove, peeled and chopped
1 tsp flaked piment d'Espelette (dried chile)
4 lemon grass sticks, crushed
2 tbsp brandy
1 cup dry white wine
4 tbsp mirin paste
3 cups fish stock (see page 324)
½ tbsp tomato paste
6 tbsp coconut cream
¼ cup heavy cream
2 tbsp unsalted butter, melted
salt
black pepper

GARNISH
slivers of fresh coconut
cooked white asparagus or salsify

Flan aux moules et jus de homard

MUSSEL FLAN WITH LOBSTER JUS

These delightful little flans can be prepared a couple of hours ahead, then set aside in the fridge until you are nearly ready to eat. While you steam the flans, you can reheat the lobster jus and warm the mussels through for a few seconds just before serving.

SERVES 4 AS A STARTER

4 lb mussels

olive oil

2 shallots, peeled and
    chopped

1 sprig of thyme

1 garlic clove, peeled and
    crushed

1 cup dry white wine

¾ cup heavy cream

3 free-range eggs

3 free-range egg yolks

6 tbsp lobster stock
    (see page 325)

2 ripe plum tomatoes,
    peeled and seeded

salt

black pepper

Scrub the mussels well. Warm a little oil in a large pan, add the shallots, and cook them gently for a few moments. Add the thyme and crushed garlic, then the mussels, and pour in the wine. Cover the pan with a lid and cook until all the mussels have opened, shaking the pan once or twice to toss them around. Discard any mussels that do not open.

Drain the mussels and set them aside, making sure you collect all the cooking juices – you should have about 1¼ cups. Heat the cream and add the mussel-cooking liquor, then take the pan off the heat and whisk in the whole eggs and the egg yolks. Pass this mixture through a fine sieve, check the seasoning, then pour it into 4 ramekins or similar heatproof dishes. Put these in a steamer over boiling water to cook until just set, 10–15 minutes – they should be firm, like a crème brûlée. Alternatively, place the dishes in a roasting pan, pour in enough boiling water to come halfway up their sides and bake in a preheated oven, at 325°F, until set, about 20 minutes.

Meanwhile, heat the lobster stock in a pan until reduced by half. Pick the mussels from the shells and cut the tomatoes into neat strips or petals. When the flans are cooked, arrange some mussels and pieces of tomato on the top of each dish and pour on the warm lobster stock.

Quiche au crabe

CRAB QUICHE

One of my favorite quiches, this is rich and full-flavored with a touch of curry heat. I like to serve it with a little grilled chicory such as Belgian endive – the slightly bitter smokiness sets off the sweetness of the crab perfectly. Radicchio also works well.

Start by making the pastry. Put the sifted flour on a clean, cold surface and make a well in the center, then add the diced butter, egg, and salt. Using your fingertips, work all the ingredients together, gradually drawing in the flour. Once the mixture has a sandy consistency, add the cold water and gently knead the pastry until smooth – but take care not to overwork it. Shape it into a ball, wrap in plastic wrap and leave it to rest in the fridge for 2 hours.

Roll out the pastry on a floured surface to a circle about ⅛ inch thick and use this to line a buttered 9½-inch flan ring. Leave the pastry to rest in the fridge again for at least 20 minutes. Preheat the oven to 400°F. Prick the pastry base with a fork, line it with parchment paper, and fill with baking beans, then bake for 20 minutes. Remove the paper and beans and put the pastry back into the oven until the base has cooked but not taken on too much color, another 10 minutes. Leave the oven on.

For the filling, trim the leek and split it in half lengthwise. Cut it into fine strips, wash these well in cold water, then drain and dry on a cloth. Melt the butter in a wide saucepan, then add the leek and cook gently until tender. Season with a little salt, pepper, and the curry powder and continue to cook for 2–3 minutes, then tip everything into a mixing bowl and let cool.

Pick through the crabmeat to remove any bones or cartilage and add it to the leek. Whisk the yolks and whole eggs, add the milk and cream, and season. Stir the egg mixture into the leek and crab, then pour everything into the pastry base. Gently place the quiche in the oven, still at 400°F, and bake for 25 minutes. Sprinkle the grated cheese on top and cook until golden and set, another 5 minutes. Remove the quiche from the oven and let cool a little before cutting it into slices to serve.

To prepare the chicory, cut in halves (Belgian endive) or wedges (radicchio), drizzle with olive oil, and season. Heat a ridged grill pan, add the endive or radicchio, and grill until pleasingly charred.

SERVES 8–10

SHORTCRUST PASTRY

2 cups all-purpose flour, sifted, plus extra for dusting

½ cup cold unsalted butter, diced

1 free-range egg, beaten

1 tsp salt

2 tbsp cold water

1 medium leek

1 tbsp unsalted butter

1 tbsp Madras curry powder

8 oz fresh white crabmeat

6 free-range egg yolks

2 free-range eggs

¾ cup milk

1⅔ cup heavy cream

2 oz Gruyère cheese, grated

salt

black pepper

CHICORY

4 or 5 heads of Belgian endive or ½ Chiogga radicchio

olive oil

Coquilles Saint-Jacques à la nage et beurre blanc

SCALLOPS WITH VELVET BUTTER SAUCE

It's always best to buy scallops in their shells so you can be sure they are fresh. And ask for diver-caught scallops, not dredged, as the dredging method damages the seabed. This is a beautifully delicate recipe that allows you to appreciate the wonderful flavor of the scallops to the full.

SERVES 4

8 large scallops in their shells
1 medium carrot, peeled
4 large pearl onions, peeled
2 celery ribs
1¼ cups dry white wine
1 bay leaf
⅓ cup heavy cream
6 tbsp cold unsalted butter, diced
1 lemon
salt
white pepper

Open the scallops and spoon out the white meat and coral, removing the black stomach and the frill, or skirt, from each one. Discard the stomachs, but soak the skirts in cold water for 20 minutes, then drain.

Slice the carrot into thin rounds. Cut the onions into thin rings. Trim and wash the celery ribs and cut them into 1¼-inch-long batons.

Pour the wine into a saucepan, add 1¼ cups water and a pinch of salt, then bring to a boil. Add the vegetables and bay leaf and simmer until the vegetables are cooked, then remove them with a slotted spoon. Add the scallop skirts to the liquid and simmer for 15 minutes, then press the liquid through a fine sieve into a bowl.

Pour half the liquid back into the pan and add the cream. Bring it to a boil, then whisk in the butter, a little at a time. Check the seasoning and add a little squeeze of lemon.

Lay the scallops and coral in a wide pan on top of the stove and pour on the other half of the liquid. Bring to a gentle simmer, then cover the scallops with parchment paper. After 1 minute, turn the scallops and cook them for a further 2 minutes (depending on their size).

To serve, drain the scallops and place them in warm bowls. Arrange the warm vegetables around them and pour on the hot sauce.

Bouillabaisse Marseillaise

FISH STEW

The name comes from *bouilli* and *baisse* – meaning to
boil, then turn down – because the fish is put into the
pot when boiling and is then slowly poached. As with
many well-loved dishes, there are 101 versions and no
consensus as to which is the ultimate. Traditionally,
whole fish is cooked in the broth and brought to the
table to be filleted and served with the piping hot soup.
My version is a little more dainty, but still remains true
to the original. The weights of the fish given are just a
guide, as what you buy will depend on what's available
on the day or in your area. Other fish that can be used
are bass, garfish, turbot, red snapper, porgy, or grouper.

Scale, gut, and fillet the fish – or ask your fishmonger to do this for you. Keep
all the bones for the stock and also keep the mullet livers, if any, to add to the
rouille (see below). Remove any pin bones from the fish and cut the flesh
into generous portions, keeping any trimmings. Rinse the bones well, put
them in a pan, and cover with cold water. Bring to a boil, skim, then simmer
for 20 minutes to make a fish stock. Pass the stock through a fine sieve.

Heat a tablespoon of olive oil in a huge pan and gently cook the onions, leek,
garlic, and chile until soft. Turn up the heat and add the fish trimmings and
velvet crabs, crushing them down in the pan with a wooden spoon. Cook
over high heat for 5–6 minutes, then add the saffron, bay, thyme, orange
peel, fennel, and tomatoes and mix well. Pour on the pastis, white wine,
and enough of the fish stock to cover well, adding a little water if you need
it. Season and simmer for 30 minutes.

Pass the soup through a food mill, then a sieve if necessary, and keep it
warm. Pan-fry the fish over medium-high heat in a drizzle of olive oil.
Serve the fish with boiled, sliced potatoes in wide bowls and pour in some
hot soup. Serve more soup on the side, and some croutons and rouille.

ROUILLE

Put all the ingredients except the oil in a food processor and blitz to a purée.
With the motor running, slowly add the oil.

SERVES 10

one 20-oz cod
1 lb conger eel
two 20-oz gurnards
two 12-oz rock cods
four 1-lb red mullets
two 12-oz weevers
14 oz monkfish
olive oil
3 onions, chopped
white part of 1 leek, chopped
3 garlic cloves, peeled and
    chopped
1 fresh chile, chopped
1 lb soft-shelled crabs
good pinch saffron strands
2 bay leaves
1 sprig of thyme
peel of 1 small orange
2 sprigs of dried fennel tops
    (or fresh fennel tops)
6 large ripe tomatoes,
    chopped
¼ cup pastis
2 cups white wine
waxy potatoes, boiled and
    sliced, for serving
croutons (see page 339)
salt and black pepper

ROUILLE
2 free-range egg yolks
½ tbsp Dijon mustard
8 garlic cloves, peeled
6 salted anchovy fillets
pinch saffron, moistened
    with lemon juice
1 red chile
red mullet livers, panfried
    (optional)
¾ cup strong olive oil

Un chef est créatif, mariant des ingrédients comme un poète marie les mots

A cook is creative, marrying ingredients
the way a poet marries words
ROGER VERGÉ

Aïoli aux légumes, buccins et couteaux

VEGETABLES, WHELKS, AND RAZOR CLAMS WITH GARLIC MAYONNAISE

This is Provençal cooking at its best – simple, gutsy food that's meant to be enjoyed outdoors in the sunshine with friends.

To make the aïoli, put the garlic cloves, egg yolks, mustard, and lemon juice in a food processor. Blitz while drizzling in the olive oil until the mixture is thick, with the texture of mayonnaise. (This can be done in a mortar with a pestle, but the food processor does a very good job as long as you don't over-blitz the mixture.) Season to taste and set aside.

Wash and trim the zucchini, green beans, cauliflower, and fennel. Divide the cauliflower into florets and leave the rest of the vegetables whole. Blanch the vegetables separately in boiling salted water until just cooked, then refresh them in iced water so they stop cooking and keep their vibrant color. Drain and set aside.

Peel the potatoes and boil in salted water until they are fully cooked. Leave them in the water to keep warm. Boil the whelks in heavily salted water for 20 minutes, then drop in the razor clams and cook for 2–3 minutes more. Drain the whelks and clams well.

Reheat the vegetables in a steamer or in boiling water. Slice them as desired, then arrange on a large platter with the seafood and serve warm, with a bowlful of aïoli.

SERVES 8

AÏOLI

10 garlic cloves, peeled
2 free-range egg yolks
1 tbsp Dijon mustard
juice of 1 lemon
1⅓ cups olive oil
salt
black pepper

¾ lb small zucchini
⅔ lb haricots verts
    (French green beans)
7 oz cauliflower
9 oz baby fennel
1 lb new potatoes
14 oz whelks
1½ lb razor clams
salt

Calamars farcis au riz sauvage

SQUID STUFFED WITH WILD RICE

This is a dish that just sings with Mediterranean tastes. I like to use lobster stock for its depth of flavor, but at a pinch you could substitute fish stock with a dash of tomato purée. Your fishmonger will clean the squid for you, but ask for them to be kept whole, with the tentacles separate.

Scrub the mussels well, then put them in a large pan with the white wine. Cover and steam the mussels for a few minutes until just done – discard any that haven't opened. Pick out the meat from the shells and set aside. Add the cooking juices from the pan to the lobster stock.

Preheat the oven to 400°F. Melt half a tablespoon of the butter in a heavy-bottomed pan that can go in the oven and gently cook the chopped onion and diced pepper until tender. Add the rice and stir until it is all coated with the butter, then pour in ¾ cup of the lobster stock. Season with the saffron and salt and pepper, then loosely cover with foil and bake in the oven for 20 minutes. Set aside to cool.

When the rice is cool, stir in the egg yolks to bind the stuffing together. Fill the squid with the rice stuffing, carefully pushing it in without damaging the body. Close the opening of each with a wooden cocktail pick. Bring the rest of the lobster stock to a simmer in a wide pan and gently cook the stuffed squid in the stock until tender, 4–5 minutes.

Transfer a few ladlefuls of the liquid to a small pan and boil until reduced to a sauce consistency.

Meanwhile, heat the remaining butter in a pan with the garlic, shallot, and parsley. Toss the mussels in the garlicky butter to warm them through. In a separate pan, fry the squid tentacles in a little oil until crispy.

Using a sharp knife, carefully cut the stuffed squid into thick slices and serve with the mussels, fried tentacles, and sauce.

SERVES 4

20 mussels
½ cup white wine
2 cups lobster stock
    (see page 325)
6 tbsp unsalted butter
1 onion, peeled and finely
    chopped
1 red bell pepper, seeded
    and diced
1 green bell pepper, seeded
    and diced
½ cup wild rice, soaked
    overnight in cold water
pinch saffron strands
2 free-range egg yolks
4 medium squid, cleaned
    and beaks removed
2 garlic cloves, peeled and
    finely chopped
1 shallot, peeled and finely
    chopped
1 small bunch of flat-leaf
    parsley, finely chopped
vegetable oil
salt
black pepper

Moules marinière

MUSSELS IN WHITE WINE

The classic mussel dish – this is quick and simple to
make and loved by all. In Normandy they use dry cider
instead of white wine, and the result is just as delicious.
Serve piping hot and provide lots of crusty bread for
dipping into the fragrant juices.

Scrub the mussels well, discarding any broken ones. Melt the butter in a
large pan over medium-low heat, then add the onion, celery, and garlic and
sweat for a few minutes. Pour in the wine and bring to a boil, then add the
mussels and cover the pan. Leave for 3 minutes, then shake the pan to toss
the mussels around and continue to cook for another 7–8 minutes. All the
mussels should have opened by this time, but discard any that haven't.

Remove the mussels with a slotted spoon and put them in a big serving dish
or individual bowls. Bring the liquid in the pan back to a boil, then add the
crème fraîche, parsley, and seasoning. As soon as the liquid has come back
to a boil, pour it over the mussels and serve at once.

SERVES 4

4–6 lb mussels
1 tbsp unsalted butter
1 large onion, peeled and
    finely chopped
4 celery ribs, finely chopped
1 garlic clove, peeled and
    finely chopped
1²⁄₃ cup dry white wine
6 tbsp crème fraîche
1 bunch of flat-leaf parsley,
    chopped
salt
black pepper

Truite aux amandes

TROUT WITH ALMONDS

This is best of all cooked with trout you've just caught
yourself, but it's always good. Serve with boiled potatoes
and steamed vegetables for mopping up all that butter.

SERVES 4

4 trout, each about 8 oz
⅞ cup all-purpose flour,
    seasoned with salt and
    black pepper
2 tbsp vegetable oil
½ cup unsalted butter
½ cup flaked almonds
juice of 1 lemon

Snip the fins off the trout and remove the guts and gills – or ask your
fishmonger to do this for you. Rinse the fish under cold water and pat
them dry with paper towels. Dust them with the seasoned flour.

Heat the oil and half the butter in a frying pan over medium heat until the
butter is frothing. Add the fish and cook them for 5 minutes on each side
until golden, while constantly basting them with the butter. Take the pan
off the heat and put the fish on a warm serving dish.

Discard the cooking fat, add the rest of the butter to the pan, and heat until
frothy. Add the flaked almonds and toss them in the butter until golden,
then add the lemon juice and pour the contents of the pan over the trout.
Serve at once.

Epigramme de sole

STUFFED SOLE FILLETS

This is a true French marvel of Dover sole fillets, stuffed with lobster, sealed in bread crumbs, and fried, then served with a rich lobster sauce. *Epigrammes* are often made with breast of lamb or veal, but this is a much more luxurious – and expensive – version. Serve with baby turnips and asparagus.

Trim the sole fillets and place them on a piece of plastic wrap. Using the smooth side of a meat mallet or a rolling pin, gently bat the fillets out to double their width. Set them aside with what was the skin side facing up.

Pull the head off the lobster, crack the shell, and remove the meat. Cut it into small dice, keeping 4 nice medallions from the tail to garnish the dish.

Heat a tablespoon of oil in a pan over medium heat and sweat the chopped shallot, celery, carrot, and garlic until the shallot is translucent, then add the lobster shell and crush it down with a rolling pin.

Add the brandy, tomato paste, fresh tomato, bay leaf, and wine, then boil until the liquid is reduced by half. Add the stock and simmer for 20 minutes, then strain through a fine sieve. Pour the strained liquid back into the pan and reduce again by half. Add 2 tablespoons of this to the diced lobster and set the rest aside. Mix the chopped herbs with the lobster.

Put a generous amount of the lobster stuffing on each sole fillet. Fold over the end of each fillet and tuck it in to make a little parcel enclosing the filling. Spread the flour and bread crumbs on separate plates and beat the egg in a bowl. Carefully roll each sole parcel in flour, then beaten egg, and finally in bread crumbs, making sure to seal the edges and keep the shape.

Warm the butter and 2 tablespoons of oil in a frying pan over medium-high heat until frothy and foaming. Add the sole parcels and shallow-fry them for about 10 minutes, turning them until golden all over and cooked through.

To finish the sauce, add the cream to the reduced lobster stock and boil until it has the consistency of a sauce. Check the seasoning and serve with the fish.

SERVES 4

2 large Dover sole, skinned and filleted (keep the bones for stock)
1 lb lobster, cooked
vegetable oil
1 shallot, peeled and chopped
1 celery rib, chopped
½ carrot, peeled and chopped
1 garlic clove, peeled and chopped
2 tbsp brandy
2 tsp tomato paste
1 tomato, cut into quarters
1 bay leaf
6 tbsp dry white wine
1⅔ cup fish stock (see page 324)
1 sprig *each* tarragon, chervil, and chives, chopped
1 cup all-purpose flour
¾ cup dried bread crumbs
1 free-range egg
5 tbsp unsalted butter
1¼ cups heavy cream
salt
black pepper

Filet de sole Véronique

SOLE WITH GREEN GRAPES

This ethereal dish is a real heirloom of the Escoffier era. Many culinary schools still use this recipe as a way to teach basic skills and techniques, and it comes up quite often in *Masterchef*. It can be made with most flat fish, such as plaice or lemon sole, but it's best with firm, meaty Dover sole. Skinning sole can be tricky, so ask your fishmonger to do this for you. They will also fillet the fish if you don't want to do it yourself, but make sure they give you the bones. The sole pairs well with steamed vegetables and green vegetables; you can serve the dish very simply with the sauce, or go to town with a more elaborate presentation for a special occasion.

SERVES 2

two 14-oz Dover soles, skinned and filleted
1 shallot, peeled and sliced
1 lemon
¼ cup dry white wine
½ cup unsalted butter
¼ cup white vermouth
2 tbsp heavy cream
1 small bunch of white grapes (preferably Muscat), peeled and seeded
salt
white pepper

Chop up the bones of the sole and rinse them well. Leave them to soak in cold water for 20 minutes, then drain. To make the stock, put the fish bones in a large saucepan with the sliced shallot, a squeeze of lemon juice, and the wine, then pour in cold water to cover. Bring to a gentle boil, skim the surface well, and simmer for 20 minutes. Pass the stock through a fine sieve and set aside.

Place the sole fillets on a piece of plastic wrap. Using a rolling pin or a small pan, gently bat the fillets to flatten them out. Roll them up – if you like, you can keep them in place with little wooden skewers.

Preheat the oven to 400°F. Put the fillets in a lightly buttered baking dish, season with salt and white pepper, then pour on the stock and vermouth. Cover the fish with some buttered parchment and place in the oven to poach gently for 5–6 minutes. Turn the fillets, then put them back in the oven for another 5–6 minutes. When the fish is just cooked, remove it from the oven and pour the cooking liquid into a saucepan. Cover the fish and set it aside to keep warm.

Boil the cooking liquid until it has reduced to a syrup. Add the cream and butter, whisking well until the liquid has emulsified into a creamy sauce.

Serve the sole beautifully garnished with the grapes, a few diced vegetables, and a little sauce, with the rest of the sauce in a jug on the side. Alternatively, pour the sauce over the fish before serving and garnish with grapes. Good with some steamed potatoes and green vegetables.

Brandade de morue aux calamars et piment d'Espelette

SALT COD PURÉE WITH SQUID AND ESPELETTE CHILE

Griddled squid goes beautifully with this classic salt cod purée, which is a brasserie favorite. The brandade is also delicious just as it is with a little toast rubbed with a clove of garlic.

Put the salt cod in a large bowl with a copious amount of fresh water and leave it in the fridge for 48 hours, changing the water at least 4 times.

Cook the potato on a bed of rock salt in a hot oven (425°F) until tender, then pass it through a potato ricer and keep warm. Drain the soaked cod and put it in a large saucepan. Pour in the milk to cover and add the bay leaves, thyme, and garlic cloves, bruising them first to release their flavor. Bring the milk just up to a boil and then turn off the heat. Leave the fish to rest in the milk for 15 minutes, then carefully flake the flesh, discarding any bones and skin. Set the milk aside.

This next part takes a little skill, as the more olive oil you can emulsify into the brandade, the more indulgent the texture will be. Too little oil and the purée will be coarse; too much and it will be an oily mess on the plate.

Start by putting the flaked cod in a food processor with a quarter of its volume of potato. Add a few tablespoons of the poaching milk and start to blend the mixture. Slowly drizzle in the olive oil, as if you were making mayonnaise, until you have a silky smooth mixture. You might need to add a little more milk if the mixture is getting too sticky or more potato if it seems too wet. Season the mixture with white pepper and possibly, although unlikely, a little sea salt. Keep the mixture warm while you cook the squid.

Empty the squid ink into a pan, add a tablespoon of the cod-cooking milk, and warm it through. Cut the squid bodies into rings and leave the bunches of tentacles whole. Season the squid lightly and cook briefly on a very hot griddle. Spoon the warm brandade on to hot plates and add some squid and a drizzle of squid ink. Sprinkle with piment d'Espelette and white pepper, and add parsley if you like.

You can make the brandade ahead of time and keep it in the fridge. When you're ready to serve, tip it into a pan, add a splash of milk and warm it through gently over a very low heat, making sure it doesn't burn.

SERVES 10 AS A STARTER

14 oz dried salt cod
1 large baking potato
rock salt
2 quarts whole milk
2 bay leaves
1 sprig of thyme
½ head of garlic, cloves
    separated
1¼ cups olive oil
3 sachets of squid ink
1 lb squid, cleaned
ground piment d'Espelette
    (chile powder)
coarsely chopped flat-leaf
    parsley (optional)
salt
ground white pepper

Dorade cuite dans sa marinade

BLACK BREAM COOKED IN ITS MARINADE

If you can't get black bream, sea bass is plentiful and works just as well here. This dish can also be served cold with salad.

Rinse the fish, dry it with kitchen paper, and remove any pin bones with tweezers. Slice the onion into thin rings and the carrot into thin rounds. Slice the fennel lengthwise into thin slices.

To make the marinade, put the wine, ¼ cup water, vinegar, juices, sugar, and cumin seeds in a saucepan, bring to a boil, and season with a little salt and pepper. Add the vegetables and stir, then remove from the heat, cover, and let cool completely.

Lay the fish flat in an ovenproof glass or earthenware dish. Pour on the cold marinade and the olive oil, cover, and leave the fish in the fridge to marinate for 6–12 hours.

Preheat the oven to 375°F. Scatter the parsley over the fish, cover with a piece of parchment paper, and cook in the oven for 12 minutes. It should be slightly undercooked and just warm.

SERVES 6

6 fillets of black bream
   (4–5 oz each)
1 onion, peeled
1 carrot, peeled
1 fennel bulb, trimmed
½ cup dry white wine
1 tbsp white wine vinegar
juice of ½ orange and
   ½ lemon
1 tsp demerara sugar
½ tsp cumin seeds
3 tbsp strong, fragrant
   olive oil
a few sprigs of flat-leaf
   parsley
sea salt
coarsely ground black
   pepper

Tagine de rouget et couscous

TAGINE OF RED MULLET AND COUSCOUS

A tagine is a traditional cooking pot, and to be true to
its North African roots, this dish should be cooked in
a tagine – or at least served in one. If you like, you can
add a few thin slices of chorizo on top of the red mullet
before you bake it.

Preheat the oven to 425°F. Fillet the red mullet, or ask the fishmonger to do
this for you, and remove any pin bones with tweezers. Cut each fillet in half
and place them skin-side up on a lightly oiled baking sheet. Brush the fish
with a little oil and season sparingly with salt.

Put the golden raisins in a small saucepan, cover them with cold water, and
bring to a boil. Drain and pat dry. Toast the couscous in hot olive oil for
about 10 seconds, then pour on about ¾ cup boiling water for it to absorb.
Remove the pan from the heat, add a little more oil, and fluff the couscous
up with a fork. Add the chopped chile (with or without seeds, depending on
hot you like your food), green onions, garlic, golden raisins, parsley, lime
juice, and season with salt to taste.

Bake the red mullet in the hot oven for a matter of minutes – the skin should
start to blister. Spoon the couscous into hot dishes and place a piece of fish
on top to serve.

SERVES 8

two 1-lb red mullets

olive oil

1 tbsp golden raisins

1⅓ cups precooked couscous

¾ cup boiling water

1 red chile, finely chopped

2 green onions, sliced

1 garlic clove, peeled and
    finely chopped

a few sprigs of flat-leaf
    parsley

juice of 1 lime

salt

Rouget grillé sur son lit de courgettes

GRILLED RED MULLET ON A BED OF ZUCCHINI CREAM

You might be surprised by the touch of curry here, but there are many French dishes that do include curry powder, especially in the south. This is a really simple recipe, but you need to make the flavored oil well in advance to give time for the flavors to infuse and develop. The recipe makes far more oil than you need for this dish, but it's a great thing to have in your cupboard and goes well with salads, fish, or grilled chicken. Do give the chargrilled bread a try. It is the ideal accompaniment to the fish, not just a decoration.

SERVES 4

1$\frac{1}{3}$ lb zucchini
1 white onion, peeled
2 garlic cloves, peeled
unsalted butter
2 tsp Madras curry powder
3$\frac{1}{3}$ cups boiling water
handful of basil leaves
4 slices of sourdough bread
olive oil
4 small red mullets (7–10 oz
    each), filleted but with
    skin left on
salt
black pepper

CURRY OIL

3 tbsp Madras curry powder
1 quart olive oil

First prepare the curry oil. Heat the curry powder carefully in a dry pan for 5 minutes to release the oils and flavor. Add the oil and heat to 105°F, then cover and let cool. After 24 hours, pour the oil through a piece of cheesecloth, then store in a bottle in a cool, dark place.

Dice all but a couple of the zucchini, slice the onion, and crush the garlic cloves.

Melt a tablespoon of butter in a large pan over medium heat and sweat the vegetables for 5 minutes. Add the 2 teaspoons curry powder and continue to cook for a further 5 minutes. Pour in the boiling water, season, and simmer for 10 minutes, then add the basil leaves and blitz in a food processor until smooth. Keep the mixture warm until you are ready to serve.

Cut the remaining zucchini into thin ribbons on a mandoline or into fine strips. Cook these gently in a little butter for a minute or so, then season and keep warm. Brush the slices of bread with oil and grill them on a hot ridged grill pan until toasted and nicely marked with grill lines.

Check that all the pin bones have been removed from the red mullet fillets, then season them lightly and smear them with olive oil. Heat the grill pan over medium-high heat and cook the mullet until just tender.

Nap each plate with a bed of zucchini cream and add some ribbons, or strips, of zucchini. Place the fish on top and drizzle with the curry-infused olive oil. Serve with the slices of grilled bread.

*Le bon repas est celui qui est
aussi agréable à la degustation
qu'à la digestion*

A good meal should be as pleasing
to the taste as to the digestion
FRENCH PROVERB

Pôchouse Bourguignonne

BURGUNDIAN FRESHWATER FISH STEW

This classic stew is made with fish native to the rivers of Burgundy. Traditionally, there should be some rich oily fish, like salmon, while the rest can be white fish, such as pike, perch, tench, or carp. Some people worry about eating freshwater species, but I think if you use fish from sustainable sources, it's fine. The dish is finished with the traditional Burgundian garnish of mushrooms and glazed onions.

Clean and fillet all the fish, keeping the bones, or ask your fishmonger to do this for you. Cut the fish into manageable pieces, bearing in mind that this is a soupy dish and is eaten with a spoon, so the portions shouldn't be too large. Blanch the ventrèche in boiling water for 5 minutes, then cut it into lardons, keeping any trimmings and end bits for the soup. Gently fry the lardons with a little drop of oil and set them aside for later. Slice the mushrooms, keeping any trimmings.

Warm a tablespoon of oil in a pan and gently cook the sliced onion with the mushroom and ventrèche trimmings until lightly colored. Add the fish bones and trimmings, deglaze the pan with the brandy, then pour in the wine and add the bouquet garni. Add water to cover, season with salt and pepper, then simmer for 20 minutes.

Meanwhile, prepare the garnish. Melt a knob of butter in a pan over medium heat, add the pearl onions, and sweat until lightly colored. Add a couple of spoonfuls of the soup and cover with a piece of parchment paper until cooked. Sauté the mushrooms in butter until they release their liquid and take on color.

To prepare the croutons, cut some thin slices of baguette, brush with oil, and rub with a cut clove of garlic. Place on a baking sheet and bake in a preheated oven at 400°F until crispy, 10 minutes.

Blitz the soup and press it through a fine sieve, whisk in add a tablespoon of butter to enrich the sauce and add shine.

Heat a tablespoon each of oil and butter in a frying pan and fry the fish until just cooked. Arrange the portions in soup plates and garnish with the ventrèche lardons, mushrooms, and pearl onions. Then pour in the soup and add a baguette crouton. Sprinkle with parsley and serve at once.

SERVES 4

1 small pike (or a 10-oz fillet)
1 small trout
2 perch
two 7-oz pieces of salmon
7 oz smoked ventrèche (see page 343) or pancetta
vegetable oil
12 button mushrooms, wiped
1 onion, peeled and sliced
good slosh of brandy (about 2 tbsp)
½ bottle Chablis or good white Chardonnay
1 bouquet garni, made up of leek, parsley stalks, bay leaves, thyme, and celery (see page 342)
unsalted butter
10 pearl onions, peeled
1 baguette
2 garlic cloves
chopped flat-leaf parsley
salt
black pepper

Aile de raie au beurre noir

SKATE WITH BLACK BUTTER

The butter in this classic fish dish is not actually black but *noisette* – nut brown – and it's important to use good-quality butter as it really does make a difference. With thick skate wings, it is best to poach them gently first, but small thin skate wings can be cooked *à la meunière* – dredged with flour and fried – and then you can add the black butter sauce afterwards. My preference is to have a thick meaty piece of skate served on the bone.

Put the onion in a large pan with the chopped celery, vinegar, wine, peppercorns, and bay leaf. Add 1 quart water and a generous pinch of salt, then bring to a simmer for 10 minutes. Allow the liquid to cool slightly, then put in the skate. Bring the water back to a simmer, then turn off the heat and leave until the skate is cool enough to handle. This should be enough to cook the skate.

Melt the butter in a separate pan, then turn up the heat and cook until golden brown – don't let it burn. Add the capers with a little of their pickling vinegar, the chopped lemon segment, and the parsley, if using. Remove the skate from the cooking liquid, drain well, and put it in the warm pan with the butter and capers for 30 seconds. Serve at once.

SERVES 2

1 onion, peeled and quartered
1 celery rib, chopped
1 tbsp white wine vinegar
6 tbsp white wine
6 black peppercorns
1 bay leaf
two 7-ounce pieces of skate, skinned
5 tbsp good-quality unsalted butter
1 tbsp capers in vinegar
1 lemon segment, chopped
1 tbsp chopped flat-leaf parsley (optional)
salt

Some of the most famous of all French classics feature chicken, duck, and other birds. Always buy the best-quality poultry you can afford, as these dishes should be a treat, lovingly prepared and richly enjoyed. There's no point working with second-rate birds. Guinea fowl has a stronger flavor than chicken and is a good introduction to feathered game, then I would urge you to get more adventurous and try others. Always keep the bones and wings of poultry to make a flavorsome stock.

Poulets, canards et gibiers à plume

Poulet sauté Marengo

CHICKEN WITH CRAYFISH AND FRIED EGGS

Legend has it that this dish was created for Napoleon after the battle of Marengo on June 14, 1800. I love the idea that his chef scoured the vicinity for ingredients and came up with a feast fit for the Emperor. It's always good to cook meat on the bone, as it retains its shape, flavor, and moisture, and this recipe is no exception.

Cut the chicken into 8 pieces. Keep the breasts on the bone and cut each of them in half, leaving the wings on. Section the legs into drumstick and thigh. Preheat the oven to 350°F.

Dust the chicken pieces in the seasoned flour, then panfry them in a little oil over medium-high heat until brown all over. Remove the chicken and set aside. Discard the oil from the pan, add a tablespoon of fresh oil, reduce the heat to low, and sweat the chopped onion until tender and just starting to color. Add the garlic and wine, then simmer for 2–3 minutes, stirring to lift any sticky bits from the base of the pan. Tip everything into an ovenproof pan with the chicken, bouquet garni, tomatoes, and stock or water. Bring to a gentle simmer, cover with a piece of parchment paper, and place in the oven for 40 minutes.

Take the pan out of the oven, remove the chicken, and pour the cooking liquid through a fine sieve into a saucepan, pressing well. Bring the liquid to a boil, add the crayfish and mushrooms, and continue to simmer until they are cooked and the sauce has reached the consistency of light cream.

Meanwhile, crack the eggs into individual cups. Heat the vegetable oil to 325°F in a deep-fat fryer, then gently tip the eggs into the oil. Cook for 4–5 minutes, depending on size – the eggs should have runny yolks and crisp, slightly colored whites. Drain them on paper towels to remove the excess oil. Quickly fry the cubes of baguette in the oil to make croutons and drain them on paper towels.

Pour the sauce back into the cooking pan or onto a warm serving dish with the chicken. Add the croutons and deep-fried eggs, sprinkle with chopped parsley, and bring to the table to serve.

SERVES 4

1 free-range chicken
all-purpose flour, seasoned
    with salt and pepper
vegetable oil
1 large onion, peeled and
    chopped
2 garlic cloves, peeled and
    crushed
1 cup dry white wine
1 bouquet garni, made up
    of bay leaves, thyme
    and parsley stalks (see
    page 342)
6 large tomatoes, peeled,
    seeded, and chopped
1 cup chicken stock (see
    page 320) or water
12 whole crayfish
12 button mushrooms
4 free-range eggs
stale baguette, cut into cubes
handful of chopped flat-leaf
    parsley
salt
black pepper

Poulet rôti en cocotte Dijonnaise

POT-ROAST CHICKEN WITH MUSTARD

Dijon is famed for its mustard, hence the title of this wonderfully simple and delicious chicken recipe. In fact, I like to use several different mustards here, as each adds its own character and flavor to the finished dish. It's always worth having a selection of mustards anyway, and they keep well. Savora mustard contains a number of spices and a touch of honey sweetness. To round out this dish, you need nothing more than a few vegetables and a twirl of noodles.

Preheat the oven to 400°F. Melt the butter and oil in a roasting pot or flameproof casserole dish on the stove top. Season the chicken, then add it to the pot, and color it on all sides.

Put the chicken in the oven to roast for 1¼ hours, but every 15 minutes turn the bird, baste it, and add some white wine until you've used up all the wine. Once the chicken is cooked, take it out of the pot and set it aside to rest.

Slice the mushrooms, add them to the pot, and cook for 2–3 minutes. Pour in the brandy and flambé briefly, then set aside to keep warm.

For the sauce, melt the butter in a heavy-bottomed pan, add the flour, and cook for 3 minutes. Pour in the milk, whisking well, bring to a boil, and cook for 7–8 minutes. Stir in the crème fraîche, then take the pan off the heat and whisk in the mustards and tarragon. Add the mushrooms and any liquid from the roasting pot to the sauce. Do not boil the sauce again, or it may separate and taste bitter.

Disjoint or carve the chicken and serve with the mushroom sauce.

SERVES 2—4

3 tbsp unsalted butter
2 tbsp vegetable oil
one 3½-lb free-range
    chicken
¾ cup dry white wine
10 oz button mushrooms,
    wiped
6 tbsp Cognac
salt
black pepper

SAUCE

1 tbsp unsalted butter
1 tbsp all-purpose flour
2 cups milk
¾ cup crème fraîche
2 tbsp whole-grain mustard
2 tbsp strong Dijon mustard
2 tbsp Savora mustard
1 bunch of fresh tarragon,
    finely chopped

Poulet Dauphinois

CHICKEN WITH FRESH WALNUTS

The sauce for this delicious chicken dish tastes beautifully creamy but is actually thickened with walnuts. It's best made with fresh "wet" walnuts, which are available for just a few weeks in autumn. These are walnuts that have just been picked so the insides are still damp and juicy, with a wonderful mild flavor.

Pour 3 quarts water into a large pan and add the roughly chopped vegetables, garlic, thyme, bay leaf, and a good pinch of salt. Simmer for 20 minutes, then let cool until tepid.

Add the chicken to the pan and bring everything to a very gentle simmer. Cook for 1½ hours, keeping the water at a slow gentle simmer – it mustn't boil – and topping up with extra water if necessary. Once the chicken is cooked, take it out, remove the skin, and cut the flesh into large bite-sized pieces. Cover them with a damp cloth and keep warm.

Add the chicken bones to the cooking stock, bring it to a boil, and simmer for a further 20 minutes, skimming off any fat and scum. Pass this through a fine sieve. Shell the fresh walnuts.

Pour 1¼ cups of the sieved stock into a blender, add the shelled fresh walnuts, and blitz to a smooth creamy sauce. Season with salt, pepper, and a hint of grated nutmeg. Pour the sauce over the chicken pieces and serve warm, garnished with toasted walnut halves, deep-fried parsley, and a drizzle of walnut oil.

GARNISH

To deep-fry the parsley, pick the leaves from the stems, wash, and dry well. Heat some vegetable oil in a pan, add the leaves, and fry for a few seconds, then drain on paper towels. Put the walnut halves in a frying pan with a drop of vegetable oil and toast them on the stove top.

SERVES 4

1 carrot, peeled and roughly chopped
½ leek, roughly chopped
1 onion, peeled and roughly chopped
3 garlic cloves, peeled and chopped
1 sprig of thyme
1 bay leaf
one 3-lb free-range chicken
10 oz fresh "wet" walnuts
freshly grated nutmeg
salt
black pepper

GARNISH
bunch of curly parsley
vegetable oil, for frying
12 dried walnut halves
2 tbsp walnut oil

Poulet de Bresse en vessie

BRESSE CHICKEN COOKED IN A PIG'S BLADDER

Bresse is just north of Lyon and famous for its chickens, which are expensive but so good and deserve special treatment. This dish is a great classic of French cuisine and one that I first came across when working for Alain Chapel at Mionnay. On a busy night we would sell 20 of these chickens and the wonderful aroma filled the kitchen and dining room alike. Cooking in a pig's bladder *(vessie)* like this is a method that cooks have used for centuries, and the current fashion of cooking meat in vacuum pouches in a water bath is simply a version of this — it's nothing new.

Pigs' bladders are sold dried, so yours will need to be soaked in cold water for a couple of hours until soft and pliable.

Remove the giblets from the chicken. Trim the neck, winglets, and feet and set them aside with the giblets. Now put a little oil on your fingers and slide slices of truffle under the skin of the chicken breast, being very careful not to break the skin. Season the inside of the chicken well and place the bird inside the bladder. Add more seasoning, then pour the stock, brandy, Madeira, and truffle juice into the bladder with the chicken. Knot the top and tie it with string to be on the safe side, then place in a large pan of simmering salted water to cook for 1½ hours. Let rest for 15 minutes before serving.

While the chicken is poaching, blanch the vegetables separately in boiling salted water, keeping them al dente, then refresh them in cold water and set aside. Trim the chanterelles so they're ready to cook at the last minute.

Heat the vegetable oil in a pan over medium-high heat and brown the chicken trimmings, giblets, and shallots, then deglaze the pan with Madeira. Add the stock, bring it to a simmer and cook for 15 minutes. Pass the liquid through a fine sieve, then pour it back into the pan, add the cream, and reduce to a sauce consistency. Keep the sauce warm.

Cook the chanterelles over medium-high heat in a little butter until they release their liquid and take on color, then season with salt and pepper. Warm the blanched vegetables through in butter.

Once the chicken has rested, break open the bladder and carve the bird. Serve with the sauce, vegetables, and chanterelles.

SERVES 4

1 pig's bladder
one 3½-lb Bresse chicken
    or any good-quality
    free-range chicken
olive oil
1 truffle, cooked and
    thinly sliced
1 tbsp *each* of chicken stock
    (see page 320), Madeira
    wine and brandy
1 tbsp truffle juice (available
    in cans)
salt
black pepper

GARNISH AND SAUCE

baby leeks, carrots, turnips,
    daikon radish, snap peas
handful of chanterelle
    mushrooms, if available,
    or other wild mushrooms
1 tbsp vegetable oil
2 shallots, peeled and
    chopped
2 tbsp Madeira wine
1⅔ cup chicken stock
1¼ cups heavy cream
unsalted butter, for frying

Suprême de volaille Agnès Sorel

POACHED CHICKEN AGNÈS SOREL

This classic recipe of poached chicken with chicken
mousse and a *suprême* sauce was created by the great
French chef Auguste Escoffier (1846–1935). He made it
in honor of Agnès Sorel, mistress of King Charles VII of
France and a keen cook herself.

SERVES 2

unsalted butter

6 large white mushrooms,
    trimmed and wiped

10 button mushrooms,
    trimmed and wiped

1 lemon

3 boneless, skinless
    free-range chicken
    half breasts, trimmed

1 free-range egg white

2 cups heavy cream

2 cups chicken stock

a few sprigs of thyme

1 bay leaf

2 shallots, peeled and
    chopped

1 cup dry white wine

¾ cup veal jus (see page 329)

4 oz cooked ox tongue, cut
    into thin rounds

deep-fried salsify crisps
    (optional – see page 338)

salt

black pepper

Heat a knob of butter in a frying pan over medium-high heat and add
all the mushrooms. Season and add a squeeze of lemon juice to keep the
mushrooms from discoloring, then cook until tender. Remove them from
the pan and set aside to cool.

Take one of the chicken breasts and blitz it with the egg white in a food
processor until smooth. Pass it through a fine sieve to remove any sinew or
gristle. Beat in about 1 cup of the cream to make a mousse that's light but still
holds its shape. It should have the texture of a thick mayonnaise.

Preheat the oven to 350°F. Butter 2 small ramekins measuring about
1¼ inches across and 1½ inches high. Finely slice the small mushrooms
and use them to line the ramekins, then fill them with the chicken mousse.
Cover the ramekins with foil and place them in a bain-marie – a small
roasting pan will do fine. Add boiling water to come about halfway up the
sides of the molds and cook them for about 10 minutes, depending on the
size. The mousse should feel firm to the touch when done. Keep them warm
in the pan of hot water until needed.

Pour the stock into a pan and add the herbs and seasoning. Gently poach the
remaining chicken until cooked through, 15–20 minutes. Keep the stock at
a simmer and do not allow it to boil. Remove the chicken and keep it warm
while you make the sauce. Set aside the cooking stock for the sauce.

Put the shallots and mushroom trimmings in a saucepan with the wine
and reduce until the pan is almost dry. Pour in half the chicken cooking
liquid and reduce by half, then add the remaining cream and reduce again.
Meanwhile, pour the veal jus into a separate pan and boil to reduce to a
sticky glaze. Finely slice the large mushrooms.

To serve, slice each chicken breast into 3 pieces and put them on warm
plates. Place some slices of ox tongue and mushroom on top and brush them
with the veal glaze. Turn out a chicken mousse on to each plate and serve
with the sauce. Add some deep-fried salsify crisps if you like.

Poulet de Bresse aux langoustines

BRESSE CHICKEN WITH LANGOUSTINES

The combination of chicken and langoustines may seem odd, but I think this is truly delicious and it was a great favorite on the menu at Le Gavroche for many years. The dish is made extra special by using a wonderful Bresse chicken if you can find one.

Cut up the chicken into breasts, legs, and thighs and season with salt and pepper. Heat the olive oil with the butter in a sauté pan over medium-high heat until foaming, then add the chicken. Cook for 15 minutes, turning twice, until golden and cooked through.

Cook the langoustines in boiling salted water for 2 minutes or less, depending on their size. Drain and cool, then remove the heads and shell the tails, reserving the shells.

Remove the chicken from the pan and keep it warm. Tip out half the cooking fat, add the onion to the pan, and cook over medium-high heat until lightly browned. Reduce the heat to low, add the langoustine heads and shells, and crush them with a wooden spoon. Raise the heat and deglaze the pan with the Madeira, then add the stock and tomatoes and cook until the pan is nearly dry. Add the cream, bring to a boil and reduce to a light sauce consistency. Pass through a fine sieve into a clean pan.

Reheat the chicken and langoustine tails in the sauce, taking care not to let it boil, or the langoustines will toughen. Serve immediately with fresh pasta if you like. Garnish with a sliced, cooked truffle for an extra treat.

SERVES 4

1 Bresse chicken (about 3 lb)
   or any good-quality
   free-range chicken
2 tbsp olive oil
3 tbsp unsalted butter
16 langoustines
1 onion, peeled and chopped
6 tbsp Madeira wine
1 cup chicken stock
   (see page 320)
4 ripe tomatoes, peeled,
   seeded, and diced
3 cups heavy cream
cooked fresh pasta, for
   serving (optional)
1 black truffle (optional)
salt
black pepper

Poulet aux lactaires délicieux et rhum

CHICKEN WITH SAFFRON MILK-CAP MUSHROOMS AND DARK RUM

Saffron milk-cap mushrooms can be found in pine forests in autumn. They're not good to eat raw as they have a bitter taste, but this disappears when they are cooked. Check them over for any grit and pine needles, then trim them with a knife. A word of warning – never eat wild mushrooms that you have gathered without being absolutely sure what they are and that they are edible.

Season the chicken suprêmes. Heat a little oil and half the butter in a heavy-bottomed pan over medium-high heat and cook the chicken skin-side down until the skin is golden. Lower the heat and turn the chicken over to cook on the other side.

Plunge the mushrooms into boiling salted water for 1 minute, then drain in a colander and pat dry with a cloth. Cut them into small pieces.

When the chicken is cooked, remove it from the pan and trim the wing tips. Discard the fat from the pan, then add the remaining butter and cook the mushrooms and shallots until golden brown. Pour in the rum, boil for 1 minute, then add the crème fraîche and check the seasoning. Boil for 2 minutes, then serve immediately with the chicken breasts.

SERVES 6

6 free-range chicken
    suprêmes, with
    wing tips and skin
vegetable oil
5 tbsp unsalted butter
1 lb saffron milk-cap
    mushrooms
4 shallots, peeled and finely
    sliced
5 tbsp good-quality dark rum
6 oz crème fraîche
salt
black pepper

Baton royal

STUFFED BUTTER ROLLS

Real extravagance in terms of work, ingredients, and satisfaction, this recipe dates back to the late 1800s. It is very good to eat and one of my father's great favorites. The filling can be fish, meat, or vegetable, but the batons must be served immediately, or the bread crumb coating may become soggy.

First make the filling. Sweat the shallot in a little butter over low heat, then add the chicken breasts, season well, and add the truffle juice, chicken stock, and bay leaf. Simmer gently until the breasts are cooked, turning them after 4 minutes. Take the chicken out and set aside, then reduce the poaching liquid over high heat. Once it's become almost a glaze, add the cream and bring to a boil, then pass the sauce through a fine sieve. Dice the chicken and fold it into the cream sauce.

Check that the rolls of butter are really cold. Cut them in half and roll them in flour, then beaten egg, and finally the seasoned bread crumbs, pressing a little to ensure a good coating.

Heat the clarified butter and the dripping or lard to 275°F in a deep-fat fryer. Add the coated butter cylinders and fry them so the interior is as golden as the exterior, 7–8 minutes. Remove them from the fat and let drain and cool for a few minutes, then carefully cut the top off each baton and pour out any hot melted butter.

Stuff the batons with the filling and top each one with some diced truffle before serving.

SERVES 4 AS A STARTER

FILLING

1 shallot, peeled and sliced
unsalted butter
2 free-range boneless, skinless chicken half breasts
1/4 cup truffle juice (available in cans)
2 cups chicken stock (see page 320)
1 bay leaf
1/2 cup heavy cream
1/3 cup cooked black truffle, diced
salt
black pepper

BATONS

two 8-oz rolls of unsalted butter (fridge cold)
4 tbsp all-purpose flour
2 free-range eggs, beaten
2 cups white bread crumbs, seasoned with salt and pepper
2 lb butter, clarified (see page 330), or ghee
2 lb clarified dripping or frying lard

Crêtes de coq demidoff

CRUMBED COCKSCOMBS WITH TRUFFLE

In France, chickens are usually sold whole, with the head, and we like to use every part. Nothing goes to waste. If you can get hold of some cockscombs, try this and you'll be surprised how good they taste.

Wash the cockscombs and pull out any remaining feathers. Put them in a pan with salted water, add a little lemon juice, and bring to a boil. Simmer until the cockscombs are tender and easy to pierce with the point of a knife – this will probably take about an hour and a half or so, depending on how big they are. Leave the cockscombs to cool in the water, then remove them and pat them dry.

Meanwhile, make the stuffing. Heat the duck fat in a pan over medium-high heat and fry the chicken livers until pink, adding the shallots, seasoning, and a splash of brandy. Let cool, then chop the mixture to make a coarse paste and add the chopped truffle.

Using a sharp knife, carefully open up each cockscomb from the base to make a pocket and fill the pockets with the stuffing. Heat the oil to 350°F in a large pan or deep-fat fryer.

Spread the flour and bread crumbs on separate plates and beat the eggs in a bowl. Dust the stuffed cockscombs with flour, then dip them in the egg and lastly the bread crumbs. Deep-fry them in batches until crisp, watching out as the oil may spit, then drain them on a cloth.

Serve with some deep-fried parsley and a bowl of Béarnaise sauce.

SERVES 4 AS A STARTER

12 oz cockscombs
1 lemon
1 tbsp duck fat
4 oz free-range chicken livers
2 shallots, peeled and chopped
brandy
1 small truffle, chopped
vegetable oil, for frying
4 tbsp all-purpose flour
6 tbsp bread crumbs
2 free-range eggs
1 big bunch of curly parsley, deep fried (see page 136)
Béarnaise sauce (see page 331)
salt
black pepper

Caneton Gavroche 67–89

ROAST DUCK BREAST, CRISPY LEGS, AND WARM LIVER PURÉE

Rich and delicious, this was one of the first duck dishes
to appear on the menu at Le Gavroche. The duck is
served two ways – first the breast, very rare and tender,
and then the well-cooked duck legs.

SERVES 2

1 large carrot, peeled

2 large turnips, peeled

3 tbsp unsalted butter

2½ cups duck stock
   (see page 322)

vegetable oil

1 Challans duck (or any
   good-quality free-range
   duck), wishbone and
   winglets removed and
   set aside

2 shallots, peeled, 1 roughly
   chopped and 1 chopped

4 oz duck liver, cleaned and
   trimmed

1–2 oz raw foie gras

²⁄₃ cup port

2 bunches of watercress

salt

black pepper

Trim and turn the carrot and turnips into 2 small barrel shapes (see page 343)
per person. Julienne the rest – keep the trimmings. Cook the barrels in
a small pan with a tablespoon of butter and a little water and salt until
tender and glazed, then set aside. Cook the julienned vegetables in another
tablespoon of butter and 4 tablespoons of the duck stock. Season and cook
until the vegetables are glazed and the liquid is reduced by half.

Preheat the oven to 425°F. Heat a little oil in a roasting pan on the stove top,
season the duck cavity, then brown the duck on all sides. Add the vegetable
trimmings, the roughly chopped shallot, and the duck winglets. Place the pan
in the preheated oven with the duck breast-side up and roast for 20 minutes.
Remove and put the duck on a rack breast-side down so that the juices flow
into the breast. Let rest for 10 minutes.

Add a good drop of vegetable oil to a very hot frying pan and add the liver, the
foie gras, and the remaining chopped shallot. Season well and cook for about
2 minutes – the livers should still be very pink. Immediately place them all
on a drum sieve and press through, adding the fat and juices that have run
from the roast duck. Collect the purée in a small pan and whisk well with a
little of the duck stock to make a thick, creamy sauce. Warm gently before
serving, but do not overheat, or it will go grainy.

Put the roasting pan back on the stove top and heat to caramelize the
contents. Add the port and the rest of the stock, then simmer for 10 minutes.
Pass the sauce through a fine sieve, then pour it back into the pan and reduce
to the desired consistency. Whisk in the remaining tablespoon of cold butter.

Remove the legs from the duck, place them in a pan skin-side up, and roast
in a preheated oven at 425°F until well done and crispy, about 15 minutes.
Remove the breasts from the carcass and peel off the skin. Trim off any sinew
and fat, then cut each breast diagonally into 5 slices, keeping the shape of the
breast. Place the duck on a hot plate and spoon the liver purée over. Serve
with the hot vegetables and sauce, then bring out the hot crispy legs and
serve on a bed of watercress and a little duck sauce.

Caneton Gavroche en pot-au-feu

POACHED DUCK WITH STUFFED CABBAGE

Challans ducks are from the Vendée area of France and are well known for their wonderful flavor and tender flesh, but you can use any good-quality duck. This is a much-loved dish at Le Gavroche and an adaptation of the richer version that was on the menu in the seventies and eighties (opposite). The new recipe, with the meat served with delicate vegetables and a clear consommé, has echoes of Asian cookery and is light and fragrant.

Trim and turn the turnips and carrots into large barrel shapes (see page 343). Clean the leeks and trim the white parts into 4 pieces the same size as the turnips. Set the prepared vegetables aside for later and keep all the trimmings.

Remove the wishbone and winglets from the duck and season the cavity. Wrap the duck up tightly in a kitchen towel or cheesecloth, then tie it tightly with string – like a parcel.

Place the duck in a deep pot with all the vegetable trimmings, the celery, herbs, garlic, and spices, then add the stock and just enough water to cover by 2 inches. Season with salt and bring to a simmer, then turn the heat down to barely a tremble. It's very important to keep the liquid just at simmering point because the stock will then remain clear. If you allow the stock to boil, it will become murky. Let cook for 1 hour and 45 minutes, turning the duck 2 or 3 times and skimming the surface well. When the time is up, leave the duck to cool in the liquid until hand hot – this should take about 45 minutes.

Carefully remove the duck. The stock should be clear and should not need clarifying – just pass it gently through a fine sieve. Ladle some of the stock into a clean pan, bring it to a simmer, and add the turnips, carrots, and leeks that you prepared earlier.

Carve the duck, which should be so tender you can spoon it off the bones. Serve the meat, white and dark, in deep bowls with the vegetables and stuffed cabbage, then ladle in some stock, sprinkled with a little tarragon and chervil. I also serve this with sauce Albert and pear chutney on the side.

SERVES 4

4 large turnips, peeled
4 carrots, peeled
2 leeks
1 large Challans duck (about 5 lb) or any good-quality free-range duck
½ bunch of celery, chopped
1 sprig of thyme
2 bay leaves
2 garlic cloves, peeled
6 star anise
2 cloves
1 tbsp black pepper, plus extra for seasoning
chopped tarragon, for garnish
chopped chervil, for garnish
1 quart chicken stock (see page 320)
stuffed cabbage (see page 148), for serving
sauce Albert (see page 148), for serving
pear chutney (see page 148), for serving
salt

STUFFED CABBAGE

Blanch the cabbage leaves in boiling salted water, then drain and refresh them in cold water. Blitz the chicken breast and egg white together in a food processor, then press the mixture through a fine sieve. Tip the mixture into a bowl set over ice, beat in the cream, and season with salt and pepper. Fold in the diced foie gras and herbs.

Divide the mixture between the 4 blanched cabbage leaves and wrap them in plastic wrap, trimming off any excess leaf. Steam the stuffed leaves over a pan of simmering water for 8–10 minutes until cooked through, then remove the plastic wrap before serving.

SAUCE ALBERT

Put the horseradish and stock in a saucepan and simmer for 10 minutes, then add the cream and cook for a further 5 minutes. If you prefer a smooth sauce, pass it through a fine sieve. Add the crumbs and seasoning and simmer for 5 minutes until dissolved and creamy in consistency. Mix the egg yolk with the mustard and then whisk this into the sauce.

PEAR CHUTNEY

Put the sugar in a large, heavy-bottomed, nonaluminium saucepan and add the apple, onion, orange rind, juice, salt, ginger, spices, and vinegar. Simmer for about 30 minutes, stirring frequently, until thick and syrupy.

Meanwhile, peel, core, and roughly chop the pears. Blanch the tomatoes in boiling water for 15 seconds, then refresh them in ice-cold water. Peel the tomatoes, cut them in half and remove the seeds, then chop the tomato flesh. Add the pears, tomatoes, and golden raisins to the saucepan and simmer until the pears are tender.

Pour the chutney into sterilized glass jars and seal while hot. Store in a cool, dark place or in the fridge for up to 6 months. If you are planning to make the duck dish it's best to prepare the chutney at least a few days ahead if you can. It's a great chutney to have in your kitchen and it goes well with all kinds of boiled meats.

STUFFED CABBAGE

4 tender green leaves
   of Savoy cabbage
1 free-range boneless,
   skinless chicken half breast
1 egg white
3/4 cup heavy cream
3 oz cooked foie gras, diced
2 tbsp chopped chives and
   parsley
salt
black pepper

SAUCE ALBERT

4 oz fresh horseradish root,
   peeled and grated
3/4 cup chicken stock
1 1/4 cups heavy cream
1 cup fresh white bread
   crumbs
1 free-range egg yolk
1 tbsp English mustard
salt
black pepper

PEAR CHUTNEY

1 1/3 cups superfine sugar
1 small Granny Smith apple,
   peeled and grated
1 small onion, peeled and
   chopped
1 tbsp coarsely grated
   orange rind
juice of 2 oranges
1/2 tbsp salt
1 1/4-inch piece fresh root
   ginger, chopped
1/2 tsp ground cinnamon
1 tsp grated nutmeg
1 tsp cayenne pepper
2 pinches saffron strands
1 1/4 cups white wine vinegar
1 1/2 lb pears
8 oz tomatoes
6 tbsp golden raisins

Charlotte au confit de canard

BREAD CHARLOTTE WITH CONFIT DUCK

This is a Roux Christmas favorite and never fails to
please. Confit duck hearts and gizzards are sometimes
available jarred, but if you're squeamish you can skip the
offal and add extra duck legs instead. You can make this
in individual molds or in one large pan.

Cut the bread into medium slices and remove the crusts, then cut the slices
in half again. Moisten the bread with some of the duck fat from the drained
confit – melt the fat and brush it on, or dip the bread into it. Line 6 small
charlotte molds with bread, making sure that the slices overlap so there are
no gaps and that they are well pressed into the molds.

Sweat the shallots with a little duck fat in a pan over low heat and cook until
soft. Add the port and reduce by half, then add the stock and reduce again
until the sauce has reduced to a syrupy consistency and is thick enough to
coat the back of a spoon. Leave the sauce to cool.

Trim the mushrooms and sear them in a hot frying pan with a knob of duck
fat. Add the chopped garlic and parsley, cook for a few minutes longer, then
tip the contents of the pan into a bowl and set aside to cool.

Remove the skin from the duck legs and shred the meat. Slice the gizzards
and hearts. Add all the meat to the mushrooms with just enough of the sticky
port sauce to bind. Season with a generous amount of pepper. Preheat the
oven to 400°F.

Divide the mixture among the bread-lined molds and cover the tops
with foil. Bake for 20 minutes. Let rest for 10 minutes before turning the
charlottes out of the molds, then serve with the remaining port sauce,
warmed through, and some extra wild mushrooms if you like – cook these
in a little duck fat.

If you prefer to make one large charlotte, use a round cake pan, measuring
about 8 inches in diameter by 4 inches deep, with a removable base. Cook
the charlotte for 35–40 minutes and let rest as above.

SERVES 6 AS A MAIN COURSE

1 large loaf of good-quality
  bread
6 confit duck legs
6 confit gizzards
6 confit hearts (optional)
duck fat from the confit
4 shallots, peeled and
  chopped
3/4 cup port
3 cups veal stock
10 oz mixed wild
  mushrooms, wiped
2 garlic cloves, peeled
  and chopped
2 tbsp chopped flat-leaf
  parsley
black pepper

*La meilleure cuisson est celle
qui prend en considération les
produits de la saison*

The best cooking is that which takes into
consideration the products of the season
AUGUSTE ESCOFFIER

Magret de canard Bordelaise

DUCK BREAST WITH RED WINE SAUCE

This recipe should be made with a fattened duck breast, which is large enough to feed two people. If you can't find one of these, use two normal duck breasts instead. The Bordelaise garnish of bone marrow is an essential part of this rich dish, along with the red wine and shallot sauce. It's lovely with some little potato cakes – see the recipe for pommes Macaire on page 174.

Trim the duck breast, then score the skin. Place the breast in a warm pan skin-side down, season, and cook gently to render the fat and crisp the skin. The breast will take about 12 minutes for pink meat, but cook it on the flesh side only for a couple of minutes. Leave it to rest before carving.

Put the sliced shallots in a pan with the wine and sugar. Bring to a boil, then add the herb bundle. Cook until the liquid has almost completely reduced, then add the stock and reduce again until it has the consistency of a sauce. Remove the herbs, then stir in the butter and seasoning to finish.

Simmer the bone marrow in salted water for 5–6 minutes, then drain. Place some bone marrow on the sliced duck and serve with the sauce and wild mushrooms.

WILD MUSHROOMS

Trim and wash the mushrooms as necessary. Heat a little vegetable oil in a pan and fry the mushrooms for 2 minutes. Drain, tipping away any water, then put the mushrooms back in the pan with the butter, chopped shallot, and garlic. Season and finish with chopped parsley.

SERVES 2

1 fattened duck breast
4 large shallots, peeled and sliced
1¼ cups red wine
1 tbsp superfine sugar
bouquet garni, made up of thyme, bay leaf, and parsley (see page 342)
2 cups good veal stock
1 tbsp unsalted butter
4 oz beef bone marrow (removed from the bone)
salt
black pepper

WILD MUSHROOMS

6 oz mixed wild mushrooms
1 tbsp unsalted butter
1 shallot, peeled and chopped
1 garlic clove, peeled and chopped
1 bunch of flat-leaf parsley, chopped

Salmis de bécasse

SALMI OF WOODCOCK

A *salmi* can be made with all kinds of game, but
invariably has a rich wine-based sauce. The sauce is
thickened with liver, or sometimes blood, and has
a depth of flavor that *salmi* aficionados appreciate.
In this recipe, the woodcocks are roasted complete with
guts, as is the tradition. The birds are then drawn and
any inedible parts such as the gizzard removed. In a
classic *salmi,* the meats are reheated in the sauce, but
I find that this overcooks the game and spoils the dish.

Season the woodcock. Heat the oil and a tablespoon of the butter in a
large pan on the stove top over medium-high heat and roast the woodcock
for 8–10 minutes. Remove the breasts and legs from the woodcock and keep
them warm. Set the heads aside.

Remove the intestines from the birds, discarding the gizzards, and chop
them finely. Put them in a bowl and beat in an equal weight of butter and
a good splash of the best brandy.

Chop up the bones of the birds and put them in the roasting pan with
½ tablespoon fresh butter and a generous seasoning of pepper. Cook on the
stove top until well browned, then add the wine. Cook until reduced by two-
thirds, then add the stock and continue to cook until the liquid has reduced
again by two-thirds. Pass the sauce through a fine sieve, then whisk in the
intestine and butter purée to finish.

Quickly cook the mushrooms in a little butter and fry the slices of brioche
in butter. Serve the woodcock breasts and legs with the sauce, fried brioche,
mushrooms, and truffle slices, then add the woodcock heads cut in half to
reveal the delicate, delicious brains.

SERVES 4

4 woodcocks
1 tbsp vegetable oil
about 10 tbsp butter
good brandy
½ bottle good red wine,
   preferably Burgundy
1 generous cup veal stock
   (see page 322)
4 oz white button
   mushrooms
8 slices of brioche
12 slices of cooked truffle
salt
black pepper

Faisan Archiduc

PHEASANT STUFFED WITH TRUFFLE AND FOIE GRAS

This is real cuisine bourgeoise – rich, opulent, and satisfying. The cooking method ensures a moist and flavorsome bird, and this recipe also works well with guinea fowl. Serve with some seasonal vegetables, such as braised cabbage.

First prepare a rice pilaf for the stuffing. Preheat the oven to 400°F. Place an ovenproof pan on the stove top, melt ½ tablespoon of the butter over low heat, and sweat the onion until softened. Add the rice and stir to coat all the grains in butter, then pour in the chicken stock. Bring to a boil, then transfer the pan to the oven and bake for 20 minutes. Remove and set aside for 20 minutes.

When the rice is cool, gently mix in the foie gras, then add the pistachios, game jus, and diced truffles. Season well.

Remove the wishbone from the pheasant and stuff the bird with the rice mixture, which should fill the cavity. Truss the bird to seal the neck and rear openings. Cover the bird with the slices of back fat and tie them securely in place. Preheat the oven to 400°F.

Heat the oil and remaining butter in a casserole dish and, when hot and foaming, add the bird and brown it on all sides. Place the dish in the oven with the bird breast-side up. After 10 minutes, add a spoonful of Madeira and put the lid on the casserole. Repeat this until the bird has been cooking for 40 minutes, then take the dish out of the oven, remove the fat, and set the bird aside to rest.

Add the cream to the casserole dish and any juices that have run from the bird, then season. Put the dish on the stove top, bring the liquid to a boil, and reduce to a sauce consistency, then pass through a fine sieve. Spoon out the stuffing and carve the bird. Serve with the sauce and stuffing.

SERVES 2

1½ tbsp unsalted butter
½ onion, peeled and chopped
¼ cup long-grain rice
⅓ cup chicken stock (see page 320)
4 oz cooked foie gras, diced (optional)
½ cup shelled pistachios
2 tbsp game jus (see page 329)
6 tbsp cooked truffles, diced
1 hen pheasant
thin slices of pork back fat
1 tbsp vegetable oil
4 tbsp Malmsey Madeira wine
¾ cup heavy cream
salt
black pepper

Suprême de pintade 'Paline'

BREAST OF GUINEA FOWL WITH ARTICHOKES AND FAVA BEANS

This is another adaptation of a great Escoffier classic. The tea gives a lovely smokiness to the cream that marries well with the flavor of the bird.

Blanch the fava beans in boiling salted water, then refresh them in iced water and remove the husks. Put the beans in a food processor, heat the ⅓ cup heavy cream, then add it to the beans and blitz to a purée. Season with salt and pepper.

Prepare the artichoke hearts (see page 342), rubbing them with lemon to keep them from discoloring, then cook in boiling salted water with a squeeze of lemon until tender. Drain and fill the artichokes with the fava bean purée. Top with a little of the remaining 3 tablespoons cream (a tablespoon in all) and a sprinkling of Parmesan and brown the filled artichokes under a preheated broiler for a few minutes.

Trim the guinea fowl suprêmes to neaten them up. Cut the ventrèche into 6 thick matchsticks. Using a skewer or small knife, push 3 matchsticks into each suprême, working diagonally through the meat.

Heat the butter and hazelnut oil in a pan over medium heat until foaming. Add the suprêmes and cook gently for 8–10 minutes, taking care that the butter doesn't burn and the meat colors only slightly. Remove, cover, and let rest.

Bring the tea and the remaining 2 tablespoons cream to a boil, then reduce to make a very thick sauce. Cut the cooked ham into julienne strips and roll them in the sauce. Serve the guinea fowl with a few drops of the cooking butter, the ham with its sauce, and the artichokes.

SERVES 2

1⅓ cup shelled fava beans
⅓ cup heavy cream, plus 3 tbsp
6 small globe artichokes
1 lemon
1 tbsp grated Parmesan cheese
2 guinea fowl suprêmes
1 slice ventrèche (see page 343) or pancetta, about 1½ inches thick
2 tbsp unsalted butter
1 tbsp hazelnut oil
2 tbsp very strong lapsang souchong tea (no milk)
2 slices of best-quality cooked ham (about 3 oz)
salt
black pepper

La volaille est pour la cuisine ce qu'est la toile pour les peintres

Poultry is for the cook what canvas is for the painter
JEAN ANTHELME BRILLAT-SAVARIN

Cailles aux raisins

QUAILS WITH GRAPES

I love the delicate flavor of quail and, prepared like this
with grapes and grape leaves, these little birds are just
exquisite. I prefer to serve quail on the bone and attack
them with my fingers, but if you want to make the dish
a little more elegant, remove the fillets and present
the meat off the bone.

Preheat the oven to 400°F. Cut the ventrèche into 4 pieces and put one
inside each quail. Place a roasting pan on the stove top and heat
2 tablespoons of the butter with ½ tablespoon of oil over medium-high
heat until foaming. Season the quails and turn them in the butter and oil
until golden, then place them in the hot oven to roast for about 8 minutes
until cooked but still pink. Remove the quails from the pan and leave them
to rest in a warm place.

Add a finely chopped shallot to the roasting pan and cook gently until
softened. Add the verjus and sugar, then the stock and simmer for a few
minutes. Pass the sauce through a fine sieve and stir in a tablespoon of
butter to finish the sauce. Check the seasoning.

Set aside 12 of the mushrooms and finely chop the rest. Heat ½ tablespoon
oil in a pan with the remaining shallot, finely chopped, and the thyme
leaves, then add the chopped mushrooms. Once cooked, add a spoonful of
the sauce to moisten the mixture. Divide this among 4 of the grape leaves
and wrap them up into little parcels. Briefly sauté the whole mushrooms in
the remaining butter until tender.

Peel the grapes if desired and remove any seeds if necessary. Just before
you're ready to serve, pat the remaining grape leaves dry. Pour some
vegetable oil into a frying pan to a depth of about ⅜ inch and heat. Shallow-
fry the grape leaves until crisp. Meanwhile, place the stuffed grape leaves
in a steamer over simmering water for a few minutes to reheat.

Serve the quail with the stuffed grape leaves and garnish with the button
mushrooms, fried leaves, and a few grapes. If you have time, try fixing
a few green and red grapes on to one stalk.

SERVES 4 AS A STARTER
OR 2 AS MAIN COURSE

2 oz smoked ventrèche (see
 page 343) or pancetta
4 large quails
3½ tbsp unsalted butter
vegetable oil
2 shallots, peeled
¼ cup verjus (or light
 white wine if you can't
 find verjus)
1 tsp brown sugar
6 tbsp brown chicken stock
 (see page 321) or veal stock
 (see page 322)
7 oz button mushrooms,
 wiped
1 sprig of thyme, leaves
 picked
8 grape leaves
small bunches of green and
 red grapes
salt
black pepper

Perdrix à la rôtissoire

PARTRIDGES ON THE ROTISSERIE

In France, this dish is cooked with thrushes in early autumn, when the birds have been gorging themselves on the remaining grapes on the vines, but in other places you could use partridges. I always serve these with a few porcini and some thick slices of grilled baguette that have been rubbed with garlic and doused in olive oil.

SERVES 4

1 tbsp golden raisins
2 thick slices of brioche
enough milk to soften the
   brioche
brandy
7 oz good-quality saucisson
   or salami
4 partridges, cleaned
olive oil
butter, if needed for
   roasting in oven
salt
black pepper

Put the golden raisins in a pan of cold water and bring to a boil, then drain and let cool.

Cut the brioche into ¾-inch cubes and douse them with a little milk and brandy until soaked. Peel the saucisson and cut it into ¾-inch cubes.

Stuff the cavity of each partridge with a few golden raisins, cubes of brioche, and saucisson. Thread the birds onto a rotisserie skewer, season, and brush with a little olive oil. Cook gently over an open flame until the skin is golden and the meat is cooked but still pink – this should take about 40 minutes, depending on how fierce the heat is or how near to the flame the birds are.

Alternatively, preheat the oven to 425°F. Rub the stuffed partridges with butter and oil and roast for about 20 minutes. The meat should be cooked but still pink.

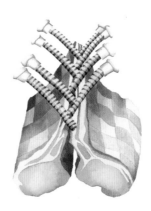

First and foremost, start with good-quality meat. Get
to know your butchers and talk to them about what
you're buying – use their knowledge and expertise.
Be adventurous and try some different meats now and
then, such as kid, wild boar, and venison as well as
the more familiar beef and lamb. All are delicious and
well worth cooking. And don't be afraid of offal. Some
of the greatest of all French dishes involve organ
meats such as brains and sweetbreads.

Viandes

Tête de veau revisitée

CALF'S HEAD, NEW STYLE

The modern method of preparing this classic French dish is lighter and more suited to modern tastes than the traditional version. Confit potatoes (see page 229) make a welcome accompaniment.

Mix the brine ingredients together. Make sure all the hair has been removed from the calf's head, then rub it, and the extra tongue, with brine. Cover and place in the fridge for 2 days.

Rinse the head and tongue well and rub them with lemon juice. Place them in a large pan with the onions, carrots, celery, bouquet garni, and most of the rest of the lemon juice, cover with cold water, and bring to a boil. Skim any scum off the surface, season, then reduce to a very low simmer and continue to cook until tender. Two hours should be about right.

Remove the head from the pan and drain, then lay it on a piece of plastic wrap, skin-side down. Peel the tongues and put one of them along the center of the head. Roll up the head in the plastic wrap as tightly as possible and place it in the fridge overnight to set.

Put the sweetbreads in a pan of salted water with a squeeze of lemon, bring to a boil, and cook for 15 minutes, then let cool. Drain the sweetbreads well and trim, then cut them into nuggets about the size of large walnuts. Dust with flour, then dip in the egg, and finally roll in the bread crumbs seasoned with salt and piment d'Espelette. Cut the remaining tongue into rectangles of about $\frac{3}{8}$ x $1\frac{1}{2}$ inches and cut the calf's head into $\frac{3}{8}$-inch slices. Heat a little oil in a pan and sear the slices until warm and slightly crisp. Do the same with the tongue and the breaded sweetbreads.

For the shallot purée, cut the shallots in half, season well, and place them in a roasting pan with the duck fat. Put them in a preheated oven, at 425°F, and cook until golden and soft. Blend them in a food processor with the duck fat until smooth.

To make the sauce, boil the veal jus, season, and add the shallot, capers, and piquillo peppers. Keep warm.

To serve, spread a generous spoonful of shallot purée on each plate and add the slices of calf's head, tongue, and sweetbread. Add some sauce and sprinkle with herbs and chopped egg.

SERVES 8–10

BRINE
2 cups coarse sea salt
1 cup superfine sugar
6 tbsp nitrate salt
1 sprig *each* thyme and
    rosemary
1 bay leaf
1 tbsp juniper berries

1 calf's head, off the bone,
    with tongue
1 additional calf's tongue
juice of 2 lemons
2 onions, roughly chopped
2 carrots, roughly chopped
4 celery ribs, chopped
1 bouquet garni
2 veal sweetbreads
all-purpose flour, for dusting
1 free-range egg, beaten
1 cup dried bread crumbs
2 tsp flaked piment
    d'Espelette (chile flakes)
vegetable oil, for frying
salt
black pepper

SHALLOT PURÉE
8 shallots, peeled
1 tbsp duck fat

SAUCE AND GARNISH
$\frac{3}{4}$ cup veal jus (see page 329)
1 shallot, peeled and finely
    chopped
2 tbsp fine capers
$1\frac{1}{2}$ tbsp diced piquillo pepper
1 hard-boiled egg, chopped
1 tbsp chopped chervil and
    tarragon leaves

Tête de veau ravigote

CALF'S HEAD, OLD STYLE

This is the traditional way to cook and serve calf's head and is still a best seller in the big bustling brasseries you find throughout France. The head is cooked in a solution called a *blanc* that is prepared with water, flour, salt, and some vinegar or lemon juice. The blanc should then be covered with a layer of fat, such as beef or veal suet, to seal the pot and prevent oxidation and therefore discoloration of the item being cooked. This is an aficionado's way of eating calf's head – very filling and not for the faint-hearted! It's sometimes made with the brain poached separately and added to the dish upon serving. It should be served with boiled vegetables and potatoes all in one big deep bowl, with *sauce ravigote*.

Make sure all the hair has been removed from the head, then put it in a huge pot and cover with cold water. Quickly bring the water to a boil, then drain and rinse clean. Rub the head with a cut lemon half.

Make the blanc by pouring cold water through a sieve into the pot and adding a tablespoon of flour per quart. Add salt (1 teaspoon per quart), 2 tablespoons of lemon juice, the onion, and the bouquet garni. Bring this to a boil, then let cool slightly. Add the calf's head, then bring to a gentle simmer and cover with a layer of beef or veal suet. You can use a wet kitchen towel instead of the suet if need be.

Cook the head until tender, about 2 hours, then let cool. Drain, peel the tongue, and cut the tongue and head meat into big chunks about ¾–1¼ inch thick – use everything, even the ears!

Make the sauce by mixing all the ingredients together. Cook the vegetables separately in salted water, then cut the carrots and leeks into large pieces.

Serve the meat piping hot with the vegetables and the ravigote sauce. If necessary, reheat the meat and the vegetables in a little of the blanc.

SERVES 12

1 calf's head, off the bone, with tongue
1 lemon
1 tbsp all-purpose flour per quart of water
1 tsp salt per quart of water
1 onion, peeled and studded with 2 cloves
1 bouquet garni, made up of leek, parsley stalks, bay leaf, thyme, and celery (see page 342)
veal or beef suet

SAUCE RAVIGOTE

6 tbsp vegetable oil
3 tbsp white wine vinegar
1 tbsp fine capers
½ tbsp chopped curly parsley
2 tbsp mixed snipped herbs – chives, tarragon, chervil
1 white onion, peeled and finely chopped
salt
black pepper

VEGETABLES

4 carrots, peeled
2 leeks, trimmed
36 small new potatoes

Blanquette de veau

WHITE VEAL STEW

A wonderfully soothing dish, *blanquette de veau* is cooked in homes and restaurants in many parts of France. Traditionally, the meat for a *blanquette* was from a very fatty part of the belly and kept on the bone. For today's taste, it is more often cooked with a leaner cut and without the bone. Rice pilaf is a good accompaniment.

Put the meat in a pan, cover generously with cold water, and bring to a boil. Turn the heat down to a gentle simmer and skim any froth off the surface. After 30 minutes, add the vegetables, bouquet garni, and a little salt. Continue to simmer for a further 80 minutes – you may need to top it up with boiling water.

While the meat is simmering, carefully decant about 2 cups of the cooking liquid and pour it over the pearl onions in a separate pan. Simmer until tender, then add the mushrooms. Cover and simmer for another 10 minutes until tender. Now drain and pour the liquid back into the meat pan. Keep the onions and mushrooms warm in a tureen.

When the veal is tender, carefully remove it and put it into the tureen. Cover and keep warm. Discard the vegetables that were cooked with the meat.

Bring the cooking liquid to a rapid boil and cook until reduced by half, 15 minutes. Add the heavy cream, boil again for 5 minutes, then take the pan off the heat and stir in the whisked egg yolk and crème fraîche mixture. Check for seasoning and pour the sauce though a fine sieve over the meat and garnish. Serve at once.

SERVES 6—8

2 lb boned breast of veal, cut into 1½-inch chunks
1 large onion, studded with 2 cloves
2 carrots, peeled
1 leek, white part only
1 bouquet garni, made up of leek, parsley stalks, bay leaf, thyme and celery (see page 342)
salt

GARNISH

24 small pearl onions, peeled
8 oz small button mushrooms, wiped

SAUCE

1¼ cups heavy cream
2 free-range egg yolks whisked with 2 tbsp crème fraîche
salt
white pepper

Côte de veau Pojarski

VEAL CHOPS, POJARSKI STYLE

In this dish, the meat is removed from the chops, minced, and then reformed around the bones. Some would ask, why bother mincing up a delicious piece of meat in this way? "Just try it" is my answer and you'll discover how delicious it is. Serve with a good meat jus, heightened with a little lemon juice. A classic dish, it may have been invented by a cook called Pojarski for Tsar Nicholas 1. Serve with some sautéed spinach.

SERVES 4

2 double veal chops
6 tbsp unsalted butter
¾ cup dried white bread crumbs, soaked in 2 tbsp cream until soft
all-purpose flour
bread crumbs
2 free-range eggs
vegetable oil (enough to shallow-fry)
salt
black pepper

Take the meat off the chops and set the bones aside. Trim the meat and remove any sinew, then mince the meat with the butter and mix in the softened bread crumbs. Season the mixture well, then shape it along each chop bone to reform the shape. Place the chops in the fridge to set.

Spread the flour and bread crumbs on separate plates and whisk the eggs in a bowl.

Dust the chops with flour first, then dip them into the egg, and lastly coat with bread crumbs. Place the chops in the fridge again to chill and set before frying – don't be tempted to skip this step, as it is important that the chops be firm before frying.

Heat enough vegetable oil in a frying pan for shallow-frying. Add the chops and gently brown them all over. Turn them carefully so that all of the crumb coating is beautifully golden – you'll need to hold each chop with tongs to brown the edges.

Meanwhile, preheat the oven to 400°F. Place the browned chops in the oven until the meat is cooked but still pink, about 15 minutes. Slice each chop in half and serve.

Cervelle de veau zingara

CALVES' BRAINS ZINGARA

Calves' brains are considered a great delicacy in France and can be prepared in a number of ways – I like to blanch the brains, then fry them until golden brown as in this recipe. *Zingara* means "gypsy woman," and to serve a dish *à la zingara* means with a sauce containing mushrooms, ham, and tomatoes.

Rinse the brains in cold water, then put them in a saucepan and cover with cold water. Add a pinch of salt and a splash of vinegar to keep the brains from discoloring. Quickly bring the water to a boil, then immediately turn the heat down to a very gentle simmer for 5 minutes. Let cool, then gently remove the brains, drain them well, and pat dry with a clean cloth.

Make sure the mushrooms are clean. Melt a tablespoon of butter in a pan, add the mushrooms and a squeeze of lemon, then cover and cook until tender. Cut the mushrooms into slices or matchsticks and keep the cooking liquid to add to the sauce. Cut the ham into pieces similar in size to the mushrooms. Dice the tomatoes.

To make the sauce, sweat the chopped shallots in a little butter over medium heat, then deglaze the pan with the white wine. Add the mushroom-cooking liquid and the veal jus, then reduce to a sauce consistency. Finish with a tablespoon of butter and seasoning, then add the mushrooms, ham, tomato, and finally the snipped tarragon. Keep warm.

Using a small knife, remove any sinew from the brains and cut them into slices. Dust in seasoned flour and gently fry the brains in a tablespoon each of oil and butter until golden brown – 3 or 4 minutes on each side. Serve with lots of the sauce and the potatoes.

POMMES MACAIRE

Preheat the oven to 400°F. Wash the potatoes, place them on a bed of rock salt on a baking sheet, and bake until tender, 40 minutes. Let cool, then cut them in half and scoop out the flesh. Mash the flesh with a fork and add the 2 tablespoons butter, cream, herbs, egg yolk, and seasoning. Shape into little potato cakes about 2 inches across by ¾ inch high, dust with flour, then fry in oil and butter until golden and hot.

SERVES 4

2 calves' brains
white wine vinegar
20 firm white button
   mushrooms, wiped
unsalted butter
1 lemon
4 slices of ham
4 plum tomatoes, peeled
   and seeded
2 shallots, peeled and
   chopped
2 tbsp white wine
1 cup veal jus (see page 329)
leaves from a bunch
   tarragon, snipped
all-purpose flour, seasoned
   with salt and pepper
vegetable oil
salt
black pepper

POMMES MACAIRE
(POTATO CAKES)

2 baking potatoes
rock salt
2 tbsp unsalted butter, plus
   extra for frying
2 tbsp heavy cream
1 tbsp snipped chives
1 tbsp chopped flat-leaf
   parsley
1 free-range egg yolk
all-purpose flour, for dusting
oil, for frying
salt
black pepper

Ris de veau braisé au safran

BRAISED SWEETBREAD WITH SAFFRON

This is one of my mother's recipes, and something she used to cook for my sister and me as a special treat. Even now I ask my mum to make this dish, and the smells and flavors take me right back to my childhood. I prefer the pancreas or "heart" sweetbread, as it is bigger and rounder and makes nicer nuggets. Great served with homemade pasta, but it's fine to use store-bought fresh pasta if you prefer.

If making your own pasta, mix all the ingredients by hand or in a mixer to make the dough. Let rest until needed.

Put the sweetbread in a pan of cold water, add salt and the juice of half a lemon, then simmer for about 7 minutes. Let cool.

Drain the sweetbread and trim off all the sinew, then break it up into nuggets. Dust in a little flour and then panfry over medium-high heat in ½ tablespoon butter and the oil until golden.

Remove the sweetbread nuggets and set them aside, then drain the excess fat from the pan. Place over medium heat and add a knob of fresh butter, then the shallots and carrots. Sweat for a few moments, then deglaze the pan with the wine, and boil to reduce. Add the chicken stock, saffron, and cream, then put the sweetbread nuggets back in the pan and simmer gently until fully cooked, basting and turning frequently. Check the seasoning, adding a squeeze of lemon if necessary.

Meanwhile, roll out the pasta dough and cut it into ribbons. Cook in plenty of boiling water, then drain and toss in a little butter.

Serve the sweetbread in deep bowls with the pasta and plenty of the rich creamy sauce.

SERVES 2

PASTA
2 cups all-purpose flour
2 free-range eggs
3 free-range egg yolks
½ tbsp olive oil
salt

1 veal sweetbread (pancreas, or "heart")
1 lemon
all-purpose flour, for dusting
unsalted butter
1 tbsp vegetable oil
2 shallots, peeled and chopped
2 carrots, peeled and sliced or diced
1 glass of sweet white wine
6 tbsp chicken stock (see page 320)
generous pinch saffron strands
6 tbsp heavy cream
salt
black pepper

Langue de boeuf au persil et câpres

SALTED OX TONGUE WITH CAPER-PARSLEY SAUCE

Tongue is a great favorite of mine and this piquant
sauce sets it off to perfection. If you like corned beef
you will enjoy this too, although the texture is different
and even more delicious. Enjoy it served hot like this,
with boiled potatoes, or cold in a sandwich with some
pickles. Keep any leftover stock for making soup.

Rinse the tongue in cold water, place it in a large pan, and cover with cold
water. Bring to a boil, then drain and rinse the tongue again.

Put the tongue back in the pan and add the carrot, onion, celery, and herbs.
Bring it to a very gentle simmer, cover with parchment paper, and cook until
tender – about 2 hours. Leave the tongue to cool in the cooking liquor and
then remove it, peel off the skin, and carve it into slices. Keep the cooking
liquor for the sauce.

To make the sauce, melt the butter in a small pan, stir in the flour, then
add ¾ cup of the cooking liquor and the cream. Cook for 10 minutes. Press
the sauce through a fine sieve, then add the parsley and capers along with
a squeeze of lemon juice if you like. Serve hot with the sliced tongue.

SERVES 8

1 salted ox tongue
1 carrot, peeled
1 onion, peeled and studded
   with 2 cloves
1 celery rib
2 bay leaves
1 sprig of thyme

CAPER PARSLEY SAUCE

3 tbsp unsalted butter
1 tbsp all-purpose flour
½ cup heavy cream
2 tbsp chopped flat-leaf
   parsley
2 tbsp capers
lemon juice

Côte de boeuf rôtie

ROAST RIB STEAK

I like my beef hung for 21 days on the bone. Most
butchers hang meat for 7–14 days, but the extra week
ensures tenderness and gives the meat a greater depth
of flavor. Fore rib (prime rib) has a vein of fat running
through it that melts as it cooks to keep the meat
beautifully moist. When you buy your beef, ask your
butcher what breed it is from, as this is important. The
various breeds, such as pure Aberdeen Angus, Dexter,
and Charolais, all have their own particular taste and
texture, so try them all and discover your favorite.
Serve with roast potatoes and green vegetables.

SERVES 2

1 bone-in rib steak
   (1–1⅓ lb with the bone)
olive oil
flaked sea salt
black pepper
Béarnaise sauce (see
   page 331), for serving

Preheat the oven to 425°F. Season the beef, then heat a roasting pan over
high heat and seal the beef all over in a little olive oil. Place it in the oven
and roast for 8 minutes – the meat should be rare. Let rest out of the oven
for 10 minutes before carving. Sprinkle the slices of beef with a little flaked
sea salt before serving.

Serve the beef with some Béarnaise sauce (see page 331), roast potatoes
and green vegetables.

Pot-au-feu

POACHED BEEF STEW

One of the ultimate French classics, this could well be my father's all-time favorite dish…or at least one of them! He likes to eat it with some *sauce Albert* (see page 148) on the side. When properly made, pot-au-feu is the most succulent winter feast and good enough to grace any table. A purée of sweet parsnips is a good accompaniment, but the vegetables cooked in the stock and the sauce are more than enough. The leftovers can be the foundation of a wonderful soup or a warm salad, dressed in a mustard-shallot vinaigrette.

Section the oxtail into pieces through the joints and trim any gristle off the tongue. Place both with the beef shank in a large pan of cold water and bring to a boil, then drain and rinse. Put everything back in the pan and add the boiling chicken or wings – if using wings, tie them in a piece of cheesecloth. Cover generously with cold water and add the 2 tablespoons salt.

Set the pan over high heat and, as soon as it comes to a boil, turn the heat down until there is barely a tremor on the surface – it should be about 200°F. Add the peppercorns, bouquet garni, garlic, and celery. Cut an onion in half and blacken the cut side on a dry griddle or grill pan, then add it to the pot with the other onion studded with 2 cloves. Continue to simmer very gently for 90 minutes, skimming when needed. At the end of the 90 minutes, remove the chicken or the wings, then put the pot back on the heat. The chicken is really just to flavor the stock, although you can strip the meat off the carcass and use it in a pie or mayonnaise salad.

Wrap the carrots and turnips in a piece of cheesecloth. Tie the cabbage and leeks together securely with kitchen string. Add these to the pot and cook for 30 minutes. Decant just enough of the liquid to cover the peeled potatoes in a separate pan and simmer until cooked. Poach the bone marrow in a little stock.

After about 2½ hours in total, the meat should be tender. Let cool a little before carefully removing it from the pan. Slice the shin. Peel the outer skin of the tongue, then slice. You can leave the oxtail on the bone or pick the meat off. Serve in deep bowls with the hot vegetables and steaming hot clear cooking stock. Serve the poached marrow on slices of toasted baguette sprinkled with sea salt.

SERVES 6

- 1 oxtail
- 1 veal tongue
- 1 lb beef shank (boned weight), tied
- 1 free-range boiling chicken or 12 chicken wings
- 2 tbsp fine salt
- 12 white peppercorns
- 1 bouquet garni, made up of leek, parsley stalks, bay leaf, thyme, and celery (see page 342)
- 4 garlic cloves, peeled
- ½ head of celery, cut from the root
- 2 onions, peeled
- 2 cloves
- 6 Chantenay or other heirloom carrots, peeled
- 6 turnips, peeled
- 1 small Savoy cabbage, cut in half
- 4 small leeks, washed and trimmed
- 6 small potatoes, peeled
- 7 oz veal bone marrow
- 6 slices of baguette bread
- coarse sea salt

Boeuf Bourguignon

BRAISED BEEF IN BURGUNDIAN WINE

Some recipes suggest marinating the beef for 24 hours or more, but I find this makes for a gamey flavor that's not entirely true to the original. Like all braised dishes, this is best eaten a day or two after it's made – simmer gently to reheat, and add the garnish just before serving so that it's bright and fresh. Boiled potatoes are the classic accompaniment, but mash is more to my taste.

Pour the wine into a saucepan and boil until reduced by half. Trim the beef and cut it into 1¼-inch cubes, then dust with flour. Heat a frying pan until very hot, add a dash of oil, and brown the beef well on all sides. Do this in batches so you don't overcrowd the pan. Preheat the oven to 325°F.

Once all the beef has been browned and set aside, discard the oil and add a tablespoon of clean oil, the sliced onion, and crushed garlic. Cook until the onion is brown and caramelized, then put the meat back in the pan. Add the brandy, followed by the reduced wine, and simmer for 2–3 minutes.

Pour everything into a cast-iron casserole dish, then season and add the bouquet garni and stock. Bring to a simmer, skim well to remove any surface scum, and cover loosely with a lid or parchment paper. Place in the oven and cook until the meat is tender – this should take 1½–2 hours, depending on the cut. Let cool, then take the meat out of the dish and set aside. Skim to remove any fat, then pass the liquid through a sieve into a pan. Boil until it thickens to a sauce, then add the meat. Cover and chill until needed.

To prepare the garnish, melt a tablespoon of butter in a saucepan and add the onions, seasoning, 2 tablespoons of the sauce from the beef, and ¼ cup water. Braise the onions until they are shiny and cooked through. Put the carrots in a pan with just enough water to cover and most of the rest of the butter. Season and bring to a gentle boil, then cook until almost all the liquid has evaporated and the carrots are tender and shiny with butter. Brown the strips of bacon in a frying pan. Sweat the mushrooms in a little butter over medium heat until cooked but still firm, then add seasoning and lemon juice.

To serve, gently reheat the braise on the stove top while you prepare the garnish. Add a couple of knobs of cold butter to enrich and add shine to the sauce, then garnish with the onions, carrots, bacon, and mushrooms. Take the dish to the table for everyone to admire, then serve in wide bowls.

SERVES 4

1 bottle of red Burgundy wine
1½ lb braising beef (chuck is good but cheek is best)
all-purpose flour, for dusting
vegetable oil
1 onion, peeled and sliced
2 garlic cloves, peeled and crushed
¼ cup brandy
1 bouquet garni, made up of thyme, bay leaf, and parsley stalks (see page 342)
1⅔ cup beef or veal stock (see pages 322–323)
2 tbsp cold unsalted butter
salt
black pepper

GARNISH

3 tbsp unsalted butter
12 brown-skinned pearl onions (or small shallots), peeled
12 young carrots, peeled
4 oz smoked bacon or ventrèche (see page 343), cut into thin strips
12 button mushrooms, wiped
juice of ½ lemon

L'ail est à la sante ce que
le parfum est à la rose

Garlic is to health what the rose is to fragrance
PROVENÇAL PROVERB

Filet de cheval grillé comme au bistro

GRILLED HORSE FILLET, BISTRO STYLE

In most of mainland Europe horsemeat is considered a delicacy, and was certainly always a treat in my family. It is slowly gaining popularity in England and I now serve it in the restaurant. This is a simple recipe that shows off the rich, slightly gamey flavor of the meat, which must be of excellent quality. Lovely served with game chips (see page 229) as well as the shallots.

SERVES 2

6 shallots
one ¾-lb horse fillet
olive oil
coarse salt
black pepper

Preheat the oven to 400°F. Put the shallots on a baking sheet and roast them for 30 minutes.

Smear the horse fillet with a little oil, then lightly season with salt and pepper. Grill on a griddle or grill pan over high heat, turning to mark it evenly all over. Transfer it to a roasting pan with a rack and put it in a preheated oven at 425°F for 8 minutes for medium rare, depending on the thickness of the meat. Let rest for 5 minutes before carving and sprinkling with a little coarse salt. Cut the shallots in half and serve them with the roasted meat.

Chevreau grillé Provençale

GRILLED KID, PROVENCE STYLE

Like new season's lamb, kid (young goat) is a traditional Easter treat in the south of France, and the milky white meat lends itself to Provençal flavors. My preferred way to cook kid is to poach it first, then grill it on a charcoal grill or barbecue. Otherwise, cook the kid in the oven and finish it under the broiler to get a lovely crisp golden brown exterior.

Place the leg and shoulder in a pan, cover with cold water, and season with salt. Add the onion, 2 of the bay leaves, the summer savory, 6 cloves garlic, the dried chile split in half, and the parsley stalks, saving the leaves for later. Bring to a boil, then turn the heat down and simmer the meat very gently for 10 minutes. Take the pan off the heat and let cool.

Chop the remaining garlic and bay leaves and put them in a bowl with the chopped parsley leaves, chile powder, honey, green and black olives, olive oil, anchovies, lemon zest and juice, and green onions. This should make a thick sauce, but add a little of the cooking liquid if you need to moisten it.

Blitz a third of the sauce to form a paste in a blender – I like to leave the rest chunky to serve with the meat. Remove the kid from the stock and pat it dry. Lightly score the skin with a thin-bladed, sharp knife and rub some of the paste onto the meat. Cover and repeat after an hour.

If using a charcoal grill or barbecue, it's important to cook the meat slowly and gently. Dip the rosemary branches into the remaining paste and use them to baste the meat regularly, until it is golden and crisp on the outside and succulent within. Over gentle heat it should take no more than 45 minutes. If cooking in the oven, cook at 400°F – the time will be about the same.

Serve with some roasted baby new potatoes and a few salad leaves. The sauce will be sufficient dressing.

SERVES 4–6

1 leg of kid on the bone
1 shoulder of kid
1 onion, peeled and quartered
4 bay leaves
1 bunch of summer savory
1 garlic bulb
1 piment d'Espelette (whole dried chile)
1 bunch of parsley
1 tsp ground piment d'Espelette (chile powder)
2 tbsp acacia honey
⅓ cup green olives, pitted and chopped
⅓ cup black olives, pitted and chopped
¾ cup olive oil
6 salted anchovy fillets, chopped
zest and juice of 1 lemon
2 green onions, thinly sliced
2 sprigs of rosemary
roasted new potatoes, for serving (see page 226)
salad leaves, for serving
salt
black pepper

*Un bon repas doit
commencer par la faim*

A good meal must begin with hunger

FRENCH PROVERB

Gigot d'agneau de sept heures

LEG OF LAMB COOKED FOR SEVEN HOURS

This is a very special dish, prepared over a time span of more than a week, but there is surprisingly little work involved and the flavor is amazing. The recipe does appear in my Gavroche cookbook but it is a great favorite and one I wanted to include here. Serve it with mashed potatoes.

Trim the lamb, remove the aitch bone, and lightly score the skin – your butcher will do all this for you. Cut 5-inch-long strips of pork back fat and use these to lard the lamb lengthwise at least 6 times with a knife or a larding needle.

Mix all the marinade ingredients together, add the lamb, and cover with plastic wrap. Place in the fridge and let marinate for a week, turning the meat several times a day so it all absorbs the flavors.

Drain the lamb, reserving the liquid and the vegetables. Heat the butter and oil in a heavy-bottomed braising pan over medium-high heat, add the lamb, and cook until golden brown. Remove the lamb from the pan and if the fat is burned, discard it and use fresh butter to cook all the vegetables (including the marinade vegetables) until golden brown. Add the bacon, then deglaze the pan with the wine, port, and marinade. Place the pan over high heat and reduce the liquid by two-thirds, then add the lamb, season well, and cover with the veal stock. Bring to a boil and skim. Check the seasoning. Put a lid on the pan and place it in the oven at 275°F for approximately 7 hours! Keep an eye on it, though, as ovens vary and you may have to top up the liquid with some water occasionally. Also, the cooking time may vary depending on the age and quality of the lamb. The meat should be tender and nearly falling off the bone.

Take the lamb out of the oven and leave it to cool in the sauce. When the lamb is cool, remove it from the pan and strain the sauce through a fine sieve. Check for seasoning and consistency – reduce the sauce if necessary. Pour the sauce over the meat and leave it in the fridge overnight.

The next day when you're ready to serve, reheat the meat gently in the sauce in a pan on the stove top, while basting occasionally. Bring it to the table and serve with a spoon – don't attempt to carve.

SERVES 8

one 6½-lb leg of lamb

7 oz pork back fat

MARINADE

½ bottle of full-bodied red wine

2 garlic cloves, peeled and crushed

1 small onion, peeled and thickly sliced

1 carrot, peeled and thickly sliced

1 sprig of thyme

1 sprig of rosemary

2 tbsp extra-virgin olive oil

2 cloves

1 tbsp white peppercorns

3 tbsp brandy

2 tbsp red wine vinegar

6 tbsp unsalted butter

2 tbsp olive oil

1 onion, peeled and sliced

1 carrot, peeled and sliced

1 celery rib, chopped

5 oz smoked bacon

2 bottles of full-bodied red wine

½ bottle of port

3 quarts veal stock (see page 322)

salt

black pepper

Carré d'agneau rôti Provençale

ROAST RACK OF LAMB

Always leave a little fat on a new season's lamb rack
to enhance the beautiful sweet flavor. Serve with a
traditional ratatouille (see page 214)and roast potatoes
with garlic (see page 226). Ask your butcher to French
trim the rack so the bones are beautifully clean.

Preheat the oven to 425°F and season the lamb. Heat the oil in an ovenproof
pan on the stove top and sear the lamb over high heat, fat-side down, until
golden. Turn the lamb over and continue to cook for another 2–3 minutes.

Add the garlic and thyme, then place the pan in the preheated oven for
16 minutes for pink lamb, basting twice. Take it out and leave the meat
to rest in a warm place.

Drain the fat from the pan, add the shallot, and cook gently over medium
heat. When it is soft, add the stock and boil until syrupy. Remove the garlic
and thyme, then whisk in the cold butter to finish the sauce. Carve the lamb
and serve.

SERVES 2

1 rack of lamb, French
  trimmed
2 tbsp vegetable oil
2 garlic cloves, peeled
  and bruised
1 sprig of thyme
1 shallot, peeled and
  finely chopped
$\frac{2}{3}$ cup veal stock
  (see page 322)
3 tbsp cold unsalted butter
salt
black pepper

Gigot d'agneau en croûte de sel

LAMB IN A SALT CRUST

Baking meat in a herby salt crust keeps it beautifully moist and brings a lovely scented flavor to the meat. The crust itself is not eaten. Serve with baby turnips.

To make the salt dough, put all the ingredients in a large bowl and bring them together by hand, then knead the dough for no more than a couple of minutes. Leave it to rest in the fridge for at least 2 hours before using.

Season the lamb and put it in a roasting pan over high heat with a little olive oil. When it is golden and sealed all over, remove it from the heat and leave it to cool slightly.

Put the bread in a food processor with the herbs and whizz to make fine green bread crumbs. Roll the lamb in the crumbs, pressing them on firmly.

Preheat the oven to 400°F. Dust your work surface very lightly with flour, then roll out the salt dough to a thickness of about ⅜ inch. If the dough cracks or breaks, you should be able to reshape it as it is fairly pliable. Place the lamb on the dough and fold it over to wrap and seal the meat completely. Beat the whole egg and egg yolk together and brush over the dough to glaze and seal the seam. Bake in the oven for 35 minutes.

Remove the lamb from the oven and leave it to rest for at least 20 minutes. Put the lamb jus into a small pan and boil to reduce by about one-third. Whisk in the butter a little at a time.

To serve, cut open the crust, remove the meat, and carve. Serve with the enriched jus.

SERVES 3—4

SALT DOUGH
1 cup fine table salt
1½ cups coarse sea salt
8 cups all-purpose flour
2 free-range egg whites
1⅔ cup lukewarm water
roughly chopped thyme, rosemary, lavender, and sage

1 leg of milk-fed lamb, boned (about 1¾ lb boned weight)
olive oil
6 slices of day-old rustic white bread, crusts removed
3 sprigs of flat-leaf parsley
3 sprigs of tarragon
all-purpose flour, for dusting
1 free-range egg
1 free-range egg yolk
¾ cup lamb jus (see page 329)
3 tbsp cold unsalted butter, diced
salt
black pepper

Filet de porc aux morilles

PORK TENDERLOIN WITH CREAMED MORELS

This creamy morel sauce can be used for any white meat, but I find it goes particularly well with pork.

Preheat the oven to 400°F. Put the pork in a roasting pan with a little oil and roast for 10 minutes, turning occasionally so it colors evenly. The meat should be cooked, but still pink and moist. Remove it from the pan and set aside to rest in a warm place while you make the sauce. Be sure to collect any juices from the meat and add them to the sauce at the end.

Discard the fat from the roasting pan and place the pan over medium heat. Add the butter and shallots and sweat until tender, about 2 minutes. Add the morels and sweat for a further 2 minutes. Pour in the Madeira and scrape the bottom of the pan with a wooden spoon to loosen any caramelized bits. Bring to a boil and reduce by two-thirds, then pour in the cream and reduce to a light sauce consistency. Season with salt and pepper.

Slice the pork tenderloin and serve with the morel sauce and perhaps some plain or wild rice or mashed potatoes to mop up the sauce.

SERVES 4

1 large organic pork tenderloin (about 2 lb trimmed weight)
olive oil
2½ tbsp unsalted butter
4 shallots, peeled and finely chopped
14 oz fresh morels, trimmed and washed
1 tbsp Madeira wine
1¼ cups heavy cream
salt
black pepper

Choucroute

PORK WITH SAUERKRAUT

This is a traditional Alsace feast. There are quite a few variations but they are always based around different cuts of pork. I have seen choucroute served with tail, snout – which I particularly love – and every morsel in between. The more mainstream versions include frankfurters, a more meaty sausage such as a Morteau, as well as knuckle or gammon and belly, all heaped over a steaming pile of pickled cabbage and cooked either in beer or white Alsatian wine. Boiled potatoes are a must. I have also come across *choucroûte de la mer* – cabbage with an assortment of seafood – and I must say I'm quite partial to this too!

Rinse the knuckles or gammon in cold water and place them in a deep pan with the belly. Cover with cold water and bring to a gentle simmer, then skim well and add the onions, spices, and bay leaves. Cook for 75 minutes, then add the Morteau sausages and continue to cook for another 15 minutes. Turn off the heat and cover the pan with a cloth or parchment paper.

Ladle out enough of the liquid to cook the potatoes in a separate pan until tender. Reheat the cabbage in a saucepan by gently simmering it with the Riesling wine and a little of the pork-cooking liquid. Five minutes before serving, reheat the frankfurters in the pan with all the other pork and serve piping hot.

Serve the meat and potatoes in big bowls on top of the hot cabbage.

SERVES 8—12

- 3 green (uncooked) pork knuckles, salted, or 2 lb green gammon (uncooked country ham)
- 2 lb pork belly in 1 piece
- 2 onions, peeled and halved
- 10 juniper berries
- 12 black peppercorns
- 2 bay leaves
- 2 Morteau, American andouille, or similar sausages
- 16 medium potatoes, peeled
- 2 lb choucroute (pickled cabbage), precooked
- 1¼ cups Riesling wine
- 8 frankfurters

Selle de lapin farcie aux pruneaux

SADDLE OF RABBIT STUFFED WITH PRUNES

This is a classic dish from the Aquitaine region, where some of the best prunes are grown, and they make wonderful brandy too. I like to serve it with a *gratin Savoyard* as well as the braised lettuce. Unless you are confident of your butchery skills, ask your butcher to bone out and trim the saddle of rabbit, keeping it intact. You also need the liver and kidneys for cooking with the lettuce.

Open out the saddle of rabbit and set the liver and kidneys aside for later. Season the meat with salt and pepper and place the prunes in a row down the middle. Roll up the saddle neatly and wrap it tightly in plastic wrap to make a sausage. Tie it securely with string. Bring a pan of seasoned water to simmering point, add the rabbit, and poach for 8 minutes.

Leave the rabbit to cool a little, then remove the plastic wrap. Heat most of the butter in a frying pan over medium-high heat until foaming, then brown the rabbit until golden, 4–5 minutes. Remove it and set aside to keep warm. Add the chopped shallots to the pan, then pour in a splash of brandy to deglaze. Stir well, scraping up all the sticky bits, then add the stock and cook until reduced and thickened. Stir in the rest of the butter to finish the sauce.

For the braised lettuce, cut the Little Gem into quarters and season. Fry it briefly in a knob of butter until lightly colored and just cooked, but still crunchy. Add the rabbit liver and kidneys and sear them quickly in a little butter until browned but still pink inside.

To serve, cut the rabbit into thick slices and place on warm plates with the lettuce, liver and kidneys, and sauce. Turn out a gratin on to each plate.

GRATIN SAVOYARD

Cut the potatoes into neat rounds. Heat the butter and oil in a pan with the garlic and herbs, then fry the potatoes until cooked and golden. Remove and pat them dry. Boil the cream in a small pan until reduced by half. Preheat the oven to 400°F. Take a couple of small chef's rings, about 1½ inches high. Starting with potato, build the gratins with alternating layers of potato, cream, and cheese, finishing with cream and cheese. Bake for 5–6 minutes, then glaze them under a hot broiler.

SERVES 2

1 saddle of rabbit, boned, with liver and kidneys
6 soft prunes, pits removed
6 tbsp unsalted butter
3 shallots, peeled and chopped
splash of brandy
1 cup veal stock (see page 322)
salt
black pepper

BRAISED LETTUCE

1 Little Gem lettuce
unsalted butter

GRATIN SAVOYARD

2 potatoes, peeled (red-skinned are ideal)
1 tbsp unsalted butter
1 tbsp oil
1 garlic clove, peeled and crushed
1 sprig of thyme
2 bay leaves
6 tbsp heavy cream
2 oz Gruyère cheese, grated

Selle de lapin rôtie aux poireaux et sauce à la bière

ROAST SADDLE OF RABBIT WITH LEEKS AND ALE SAUCE

This is a traditional robust country dish, full of great flavors. I like to cook and serve the rabbit on the bone — it might not look very elegant, but the meat stays tender and juicy. The kidneys should be attached to the saddles, so just leave them on to cook with the rabbit.

Bring a pan of salted water to a boil. Blanch the leeks until tender, then remove and refresh them in iced water. Drain and slice them into rounds about ³⁄₈ inch thick.

Preheat the oven to 425°F. Heat a tablespoon of oil in a cast-iron casserole dish over medium-high heat and brown the seasoned rabbit until golden on all sides. Add a tablespoon of butter and the onion, then place the casserole dish in the oven for 15 minutes. Remove the rabbit saddles from the dish and leave them to rest in a warm place.

Put the casserole dish back on the stove and pour in the ale, lemon juice, and moalsses. Boil until almost dry, then add the stock and simmer for 10 minutes.

Whisk a tablespoon of butter into the sauce, then pass it through a fine sieve and season to taste. Panfry the leeks in a nonstick pan with a little oil and butter until brown, or brown them on a ridged grill pan. Serve the rabbit with the leeks, sauce, and roast potatoes.

SERVES 4

2 large leeks, trimmed and cleaned (or baby leeks in season)

vegetable oil

4 saddles of rabbit, on the bone with kidneys

unsalted butter

1 medium onion, peeled and sliced

6 tbsp good brown ale

1 tbsp lemon juice

1 tbsp molasses

¾ cup chicken stock (see page 320)

roasted potatoes, for serving (see page 226)

salt

black pepper

Carpaccio de chevreuil

VENISON CARPACCIO

Carpaccio is Italian in origin, but we have a tradition of serving raw meat in France and we've taken this dish to our hearts. It's an excellent way to serve good venison and extremely easy to prepare. The most difficult part is slicing the meat really thinly. You'll need a good sharp knife or a slicing machine – a piece of kit that's readily available now, not too expensive and useful for a number of tasks. If you don't have time to freeze the meat, put it in the freezer until firm and almost frozen, then remove and slice.

Check that your venison has been nicely trimmed and there are no traces of fat or sinew. Freeze the venison, then take it out of the freezer about half an hour before you want to serve.

Shave the vegetables into fine strips using a Japanese mandoline, then place them in iced water to curl and crisp. To make the horseradish cream, whip the cream until firm and fold in the horseradish and a pinch of salt. Whisk the ingredients for the dressing together.

Cut the meat as thinly as possible and arrange overlapping slices on each plate.

Drain the vegetables well and add some to each plate along with the cheese and a spoonful of horseradish cream. Drizzle with the dressing and sprinkle over the mixed shoots.

SERVES 4 AS A STARTER

one 12-oz tenderloin of
  venison (trimmed weight)
2 small turnips, peeled
4 breakfast radishes
4 thin slices of Berkswell
  sheep's milk cheese
  (or pecorino)
mixed herb shoots

HORSERADISH CREAM
6 tbsp whipping cream
2 oz fresh horseradish root,
  peeled and grated
salt

DRESSING
1 tbsp balsamic vinegar
2 tbsp olive oil
salt
black pepper

Gigue de chevreuil rôtie à la Chevigné

ROAST LEG OF VENISON WITH PEARS, CHESTNUTS AND PEPPER SAUCE

Venison is available almost all year round and it's a great alternative to beef for a family roast. I think it's best in the winter months, and this rich pepper sauce is a classic accompaniment. You need to start this dish well before you want to eat it, as the meat has to marinate for two days.

To make the marinade, crush the juniper berries, peppercorns, and bay leaves in a mortar with a pestle and add the olive oil, wine, and brandy. Using a larding needle, thread the strips of pork fat evenly through the venison. If you don't have a needle, make cuts with a long thin knife and push the fat into them with your finger. Put the meat in a plastic bag with the marinade, seal, and refrigerate for 2 days, turning and massaging it occasionally.

To make the sauce, warm the oil in a frying pan and cook the shallots until caramelized. Add the peppercorns and red currant jelly and stir until the jelly has melted, then pour in the vinegar and let it boil away. Pour in the wine and port and cook until the liquid is reduced by half. Add the stock and reduce by half again, then pass the sauce through a fine sieve into a clean pan. Season, place over medium heat, and whisk in 2 tablespoons of butter.

For the garnish, heat 2 tablespoons of the butter until foaming, then add the pears and cook them gently until golden and tender. Drain off a little of the butter, then add the honey to give the pears a gloss and shine. Finish with a squeeze of lemon juice and season with salt and pepper.

Preheat the oven to 400°F and bake the shallots for 20 minutes, then let cool. Remove the skins and cut the shallots in half, then fry them in a nonstick pan with a tablespoon of butter until golden and caramelized. Season. Bring the cream to a boil, add the chestnuts, then blitz in a blender until smooth. Add the remaining 2 tablepoons of butter to add gloss to the purée. Season as necessary.

Take the meat out of the fridge at least an hour before cooking. Preheat the oven to 450°F. Drain the venison, place it in a roasting pan, and rub the oil into the meat. Season well and put it in the oven. After 20 minutes, turn the heat down to 400°F and continue to cook for 40 minutes for pink meat. Remove the venison and let rest for at least 20 minutes before carving and serving with the hot sauce, garnished with the cooked pears, shallots, and chestnut purée.

SERVES 6

4 juniper berries
6 black peppercorns
2 bay leaves
2 tbsp olive oil
6 tbsp red wine
2 tbsp brandy
7 oz pork back fat, cut into long strips about ¼ inch thick
one 8-lb leg of venison on the bone
2 tbsp vegetable oil

SAUCE POIVRADE
(PEPPER SAUCE)

1 tbsp vegetable oil
6 shallots, peeled and sliced
1 tbsp crushed white and black peppercorns
1 tbsp red currant jelly
3 tbsp red wine vinegar
1¼ cups full-bodied red wine
6 tbsp port
2½ cups game stock
2 tbsp unsalted butter

GARNISH

5 tbsp unsalted butter
4 Comice pears, peeled and quartered
2 tbsp honey
1 lemon
8–12 shallots
½ cup heavy cream
7 oz cooked chestnuts (vacuum packed are fine)
salt
black pepper

Cuisine n'est pas chimie. C'est un art. Elle exige instinct et le goût plutôt que des mesures exactes

Cooking is not chemistry. It is an art. It requires instinct and taste rather than exact measurements

MARCEL BOULESTIN

Epaule de sanglier braisée, crème de cassis pimentée

BRAISED SHOULDER OF WILD BOAR WITH PEPPERED CASSIS SAUCE

There are now wild boar all over France, even in the suburbs of some major cities. The meat is delicious when slow cooked, and I particularly enjoy the shoulder on the bone. I have a regular supply of wild boar from my brother-in-law Gérard, who shoots them in the Cévennes hills. Farmed boar is now available from many butchers and tastes good, but might not need to be cooked for quite so long. Start this the day before you want to eat it, as the meat needs to marinate for 24 hours. Barley risotto makes an excellent accompaniment.

SERVES 6

one 8- to 10-lb wild boar
   shoulder
3 tbsp red wine vinegar
3 tbsp brandy
3 tbsp olive oil
2 bay leaves
2 piments d'Espelette
   (whole dried chiles),
   cut in half
8 garlic cloves, peeled
2 onions, peeled and sliced
¾ cup crème de cassis
barley risotto, for serving
   (see page 251)
salt
black pepper

Make small incisions with a sharp knife all over the boar shoulder. Place it in a plastic bag and add the vinegar, brandy, oil, bay leaves, and piments d'Espelette. Seal the bag and leave the meat to marinate in the fridge for 24 hours.

When you're ready to cook, preheat the oven to 425°F. Take the meat out of the bag and drain off the marinade – set it aside for later, including the chiles and bay. Season the meat, place it in a roasting pan, and put it in the preheated oven for 30 minutes. Then add the peeled garlic, sliced onions, the marinade, and crème de cassis, turn the oven down to 325°F and cook for a further 10 minutes. Add 1¼ cups water, cover loosely with foil, and continue to cook until the meat is tender and falling off the bone, a further 4 hours.

The cooking liquid should be of sauce consistency, but if not, transfer it to a pan and boil until reduced and syrupy. You may need to skim off a little fat. I prefer to leave the garlic, onions, and chile in the sauce, but if you want it silky smooth, press it through a fine sieve. Carve the meat and serve with the sauce and barley risotto.

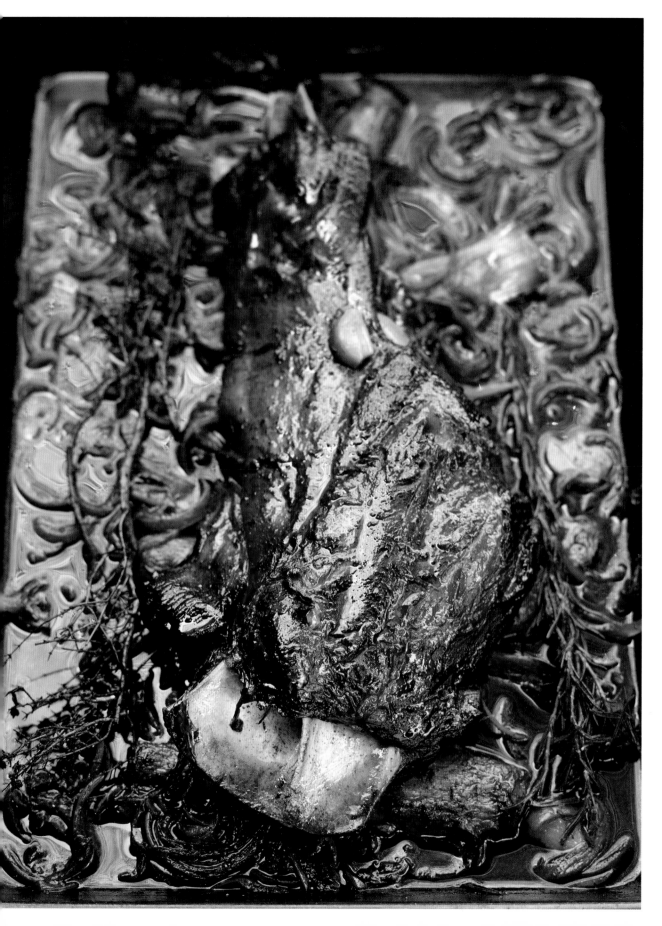

Tête de sanglier sauce mousquetaire

CRISPY WILD BOAR HEAD WITH SPICY SHALLOT MAYONNAISE

This can also be made with ordinary pork, but it's particularly good with wild boar. The head needs to be shaved and singed to remove all the bristles, then taken off the bone. If this is beyond your talents, the butcher should be able to oblige. Serve with roast vegetables.

Take the head, lay it out flat, skin-side down, on your work surface, and season. Mix the garlic, mustard, rosemary, and thyme and spread this evenly over the meat. Then roll the head up neatly and tie tightly with string. Place it in a pan, cover well with cold water, and bring it to a boil. Skim well, add the celery, carrot, onion, bay, peppercorns, and some salt, then turn down the heat so the water is barely simmering. Cook gently for 2–3 hours, depending on the size of the head, until the meat is tender and easily pierced with a skewer.

Leave the meat to cool in the cooking liquid, then take it out and roll it tightly in plastic wrap. Refrigerate overnight. Pass the stock through a sieve and use it for a soup another time.

For the sauce, simmer the finely chopped shallots in the wine until all the liquid has evaporated. Add the stock and continue to cook until the shallots are soft and the liquid sticky. Season with salt, pepper, and a generous amount of cayenne, then leave it to cook a little.

Make a mayonnaise by combining the yolks, mustard, and vinegar and slowly whisking in the oil. Once made, add the shallot mix and check the seasoning. The sauce should have a good kick and be a little sharp.

When you're ready to eat, cut the head into ¾-inch slices and then remove the string and plastic wrap – they help to keep everything in place as you slice. Heat a tablespoon of vegetable oil and fry the slices until crispy on both sides. Serve with the mayonnaise.

SERVES 10–12

1 wild boar head, 4–6 lb boned weight
1 garlic clove, peeled and very finely chopped
1 tbsp whole-grain Dijon mustard
1 tbsp mixed chopped rosemary and thyme leaves
1 celery rib
1 carrot, peeled
1 onion, peeled
2 bay leaves
1 tbsp black peppercorns
1 tbsp vegetable oil
salt

SPICY SHALLOT MAYONNAISE
2 shallots, peeled and finely chopped
½ cup dry white wine
½ cup veal stock (see page 322)
good pinch cayenne pepper
2 free-range egg yolks
1 tbsp Dijon mustard
1 tbsp white wine vinegar
1 cup vegetable oil
salt
black pepper

Escargots à la Chartreuse et noisettes

SNAILS WITH CHARTREUSE AND HAZELNUTS

I remember being dragged out into the fields with my father and mother to collect snails after a heavy shower. We purged (fasted) the snails for several days and washed them in copious amounts of salted water. They then had to be boiled, removed from the shell, intestines trimmed off, and finally bottled and preserved for later use. Thankfully you can now buy jars or cans of very good-quality precooked snails, with all the hard work already done – though I look back on those days with much fondness.

SERVES 6 AS A STARTER

6 dozen snails (canned are fine)
3 shallots, peeled and finely chopped
3 garlic cloves, peeled and finely chopped
2 tbsp olive oil
3 tbsp chopped hazelnuts
1½ tbsp unsalted butter
2 tbsp green Chartreuse
2 cups whipping cream
lemon juice
grated lemon zest
2 tbsp chopped parsley
salt
black pepper

Drain the snails. Sweat the finely chopped shallots and garlic in the olive oil over medium heat until tender, then add the hazelnuts, followed by the snails. Add the butter and continue to cook gently for 6–7 minutes.

Pour in the Chartreuse, turn up the heat, and boil until the pan is almost dry. Add the cream and simmer until the mixture has the consistency of a sauce. Season well and finish with a few drops of lemon juice and a little finely grated zest. Serve in little pots with a sprinkling of parsley.

Vegetables are treated with proper care and respect
in the French kitchen. Not only do they partner fish
or meat, but they can also be the stars of many dishes
and the basis of a whole meal. Seasonality is all-
important. Go to the market in a French town, and
you will find vegetables that are grown in the region,
rather than items imported from many different
parts of the world. Salads are not just for garnish and
can be stand-alone dishes – try the smoked duck
and cabbage on page 248, for example. Lighter salads
are usually served after the main course.

Légumes et salades

Ratatouille

MEDITERRANEAN VEGETABLE STEW

For this Provençal dish to taste its best, all the
vegetables must be cooked separately before being
combined for the final stage. All too often ratatouille
is an indeterminate mush, but when properly prepared
with ingredients at the peak of their summery
perfection, it can be a joy. Delicious warm or cold –
lovely served with rack of lamb (see page 192).

SERVES 4

1 eggplant

2 zucchini

1 red bell pepper, peeled
  and seeded

1 large onion, peeled

2 tomatoes, peeled and
  seeded

olive oil

1 bulb green garlic, chopped

1 sprig thyme

2 bay leaves

2 tbsp tomato paste

salt

black pepper

Dice the eggplant, zucchini, pepper, onion and tomatoes – large or small, as
you prefer – keeping them in separate piles. Heat about ⅜ inch olive oil in
a pan over high heat and color each type of vegetable, except the tomatoes,
individually, then drain them in a colander.

Preheat the oven to 400°F. Place all the vegetables in an ovenproof dish or
large pan and add the diced tomatoes, garlic, thyme, bay leaves, and tomato
paste. Season and cover with parchment paper. Place in the preheated oven
for about 20 minutes or so until all the vegetables are tender. If you prefer,
you can do this on the stove top over a gentle heat.

Gâteau Savoyard aux pommes de terre et lard

POTATO, PRUNE, AND BACON CAKE

A traditional country-style recipe from the
Savoie region of France, this can be served as an
accompaniment for a roast or as a stand-alone dish
with dandelion salad. Some recipes use prunes, others
golden raisins, but I like to include both. The shape
is important not only for presentation but also for the
cooking. Traditionally, this is baked in a Kugelhopf
mold or the fluted mold for the sweet gâteau de Savoie,
but you can use an ordinary 8-inch cake pan.

SERVES 6

3 lb baking potatoes
2 onions, peeled and finely
    sliced
16 plump soft prunes, pitted
6 tbsp golden raisins
26 thin slices bacon
unsalted butter, for greasing
salt
black pepper

Peel the potatoes and grate them coarsely, then place them in a cloth and
squeeze them dry. Tip the grated potatoes into a bowl, then add the finely
sliced onions, prunes, golden raisins, and a generous amount of seasoning
and mix together well.

Preheat the oven to 350°F. Line the mold with the bacon rashers, making
sure they overlap a little and hang over the sides of the mold. Pack in the
potato mixture and fold the overhanging bacon over the top. Place the mold
in a bain-marie or a roasting pan and pour in enough boiling water to come
halfway up the sides. Cover with some buttered foil and bake for 2 hours.

Allow the gâteau to cool a little before turning it out of the mold — it will fall
apart if you try to turn it out right away. Wonderful hot or cold.

Gratin de macaronis au potiron

BAKED MACARONI WITH SQUASH

Use butternut or any other kind of winter squash to
make this dish, which goes beautifully with roast game
and other meats or can be served on its own. Meat stock
is best as it helps to glue the pasta together, but you
could use vegetable stock to make a vegetarian version.

Preheat the oven to 400°F. Put the squash in a baking sheet, drizzle it with
olive oil, and bake in the oven until tender, about 30 minutes. Scrape all
the flesh off the skin and mash it with a fork, then season well and add the
crushed amaretti.

For cooking the macaroni you need a pan large enough to hold all the pieces
in a single layer. Heat the butter in the pan until it is foaming, then add the
macaroni. Roll the pasta in the butter until it is golden on all sides, then
add the stock and bring to a simmer. Season and continue to cook until the
pasta is tender and the stock has almost completely evaporated; add a little
water if necessary.

Place the macaroni side by side on a piece of parchment paper – it's
important that they be tightly packed together – and smear any liquid
that's left over the top. Put them in the fridge for about an hour to set. Once
set, cut the macaroni into 8 small rounds about 3 inches across, or to fit
the dishes or chef's rings you are going to use. Boil the cream until it
thickens, then season with salt and pepper.

Preheat the oven to 400°F. Place 4 dishes or chef's rings on a baking sheet
and place a circle of macaroni in each one, followed by some squash and
a generous amount of cream. Repeat the layers, finishing with a circle of
macaroni, then top with cream, grated Parmesan, and chopped almonds.
Bake for about 10 minutes to reheat, then color the top under a hot broiler.
Carefully remove from the dishes or rings and serve the gratins as an
accompaniment to a main course or as a starter with a few bitter salad leaves.

SERVES 4

1 1/2 lb mixed squash, cut into
    wedges
olive oil
6 amaretto cookies, crushed
1/2 lb dried macaroni
1/4 cup unsalted butter
1 1/4 cups veal stock
    (see page 322)
3/4 cup heavy cream
6 tbsp Parmesan cheese,
    grated
1/4 cup salted almonds,
    chopped
salt
black pepper

Salade Lyonnaise

DANDELION AND BACON SALAD

The classic *salade lyonnaise* is made with dandelion
leaves, and if you are lucky enough to have a garden
with an untreated area in it, you can pick your own.
However, dandelions can taste a little overly bitter to
some people, so you can use frisée salad or curly endive
if you prefer.

SERVES 6

14 oz dandelion leaves or
    other bitter salad greens
6 oz smoked bacon
4 tbsp olive oil
1 small baguette
2 garlic cloves
white wine vinegar
6 free-range eggs
2 tbsp red wine vinegar
salt
black pepper

Pick through the salad leaves, then wash and dry them carefully. Cut the
bacon into strips or batons, place them in a nonstick pan with a drop of
olive oil, and cook slowly over medium heat.

Cut the baguette into about 20 slices, ³⁄₈ inch thick. Drizzle them with olive
oil, then bake in a preheated oven at 400°F until crisp, about 15 minutes.
Rub with a cut clove of garlic.

Put a saucepan of water on to boil with a generous splash of white wine
vinegar. Crack the eggs and carefully drop them into the simmering
vinegared water to poach, reducing the heat as needed to cook them gently.
The eggs should take about 4 minutes for the whites to be cooked, but the
yolks should still be runny.

Put the salad leaves in a bowl and pour the golden-brown bacon and fat on
top. Add the toasts, red wine vinegar, and remaining olive oil, season lightly
with salt but generously with pepper, then toss. Arrange the salad on plates
and place the drained, hot eggs on top. Serve immediately.

Artichauts vinaigrette

ARTICHOKES VINAIGRETTE

Globe artichokes were a real treat for me as a child, but I remember my English friends coming round for dinner and being quite scared when they saw these alien things on the plate. I loved the sheer delight and fun of tearing off the leaves, dipping them into the vinaigrette, and finally drawing the leaf through clenched teeth to scrape away a morsel of deliciously deep-flavored artichoke. When all the leaves have been chewed, only the heart and the inedible choke is left. This needs to be lifted or scraped out with a spoon. Add another drizzle of vinaigrette, and one of the most classic and satisfying starters is complete.

SERVES 4

4 large globe artichokes
pinch salt
1 lemon, cut into quarters

VINAIGRETTE

2 tbsp olive oil
6 tbsp vegetable oil
2 tsp Dijon mustard
2 tbsp white wine vinegar
salt
black pepper

Trim off the stems and place the artichokes in a deep pan. Cover with cold water and add a pinch of salt and the lemon quarters. Bring the water to a boil and simmer the artichokes gently for 30–40 minutes. You may need to put a plate on top of the artichokes to keep them submerged. Take the artichokes out of the water and drain, then check they are done by pulling off a couple of leaves.

Whisk all the vinaigrette ingredients together and serve with the artichokes. I think they are best served warm, but you can put them in the fridge and eat them the next day.

Je veux l'ordre et le goût. Un repas bien affiché est renforcé à cent pour cent à mes yeux

I want order and taste. A well-displayed meal is enhanced one hundred percent in my eyes

ANTONIN CARÊME

Pommes de terre rôties à l'ail

ROAST POTATOES WITH GARLIC

I like to use a cast-iron pan for cooking these potatoes
(opposite), which go perfectly with a rack of lamb.

Scrub and drain the potatoes well. Heat the oil in a cast-iron pan until
smoking, then add the potatoes. Cook until light golden brown all over, then
add the garlic, thyme, and butter. Turn down the heat and loosely cover the
potatoes with parchment paper, then cook gently until tender, 10 minutes.
Season, drain off the fat, and tip the potatoes into a bowl to serve.

SERVES 4

6 oz small new potatoes,
    peeled
2 tbsp vegetable oil
6 garlic cloves
a few sprigs of thyme
1 tbsp unsalted butter
salt
black pepper

Pommes boulangère

POTATOES COOKED WITH STOCK AND ONIONS

This dish is named after the baker because the tradition
was to cook it in the bakery oven once all the bread was
done. The residual heat ensured a lovely long and slow
cooking time for this delicious potato dish. Excellent
served with roast pork or white meats.

Peel the potatoes and cut them into slices about $^1/_{16}$–$^1/_8$ inch thick. Do not
wash them. Peel and thinly slice the onions. Heat the oil and a tablespoon
of the butter in a frying pan over medium heat, add the onions, and fry until
soft but not colored. Add them to the potatoes, season well, and spread
everything in an ovenproof dish. Preheat the oven to 400°F.

Pour the stock into the dish, add the thyme, and place in the oven for
35 minutes. Melt the remaining butter. Take the dish out, press down on
the potatoes with a slotted spoon, then brush the tops with the melted
butter. Put the potatoes back in the oven for 10 minutes to crisp up.

SERVES 8

2 lb red-skinned potatoes
2–3 onions
1 tbsp vegetable oil
2 tbsp unsalted butter
1 cup chicken stock
    (see page 320)
1 sprig thyme
salt
black pepper

Pommes gaufrettes

GAME CHIPS

These crispy waffle-style chips (*opposite*) can be cut on
a mandoline with a waffle blade. Perfect with good plain
meat such as grilled fillet of horse (see page 187).

Peel the potatoes, then slice them as thinly as possible on a mandoline.
Rinse in cold water, then drain and pat dry.

Heat the duck fat or dripping in a deep-fat fryer or large pot to 325°F and
fry the game chips a batch at a time until golden and crispy. Drain and season
with a little salt.

SERVES 2–3

2–3 all-purpose potatoes,
    such as red-skinned
2 lb duck fat or dripping,
    for frying
salt

Pommes de terre confites

GRILLED POTATOES COOKED IN DUCK FAT

Confit potatoes, slowly cooked in delicious duck fat,
go beautifully with tête de veau revisitée (see page 168),
among other dishes.

Peel the potatoes and, using a sharp knife, trim them into cylinder shapes
with a flat top and bottom. Cook them briefly on a hot ridged grill until they
are nicely marked with the grill lines.

Melt the duck fat in a pan over medium-low heat and add the potatoes – they
should be submerged in the fat. Cook until tender, about 25 minutes. Season
with a little salt.

SERVES 6–8

8 all-purpose potatoes,
    such as Yellow Finn or
    red-skinned
7 oz duck fat
salt

Ragoût de morilles

MOREL AND CELERY ROOT STEW

For me, morel mushrooms are the best of all mushrooms. When they're out of season I use the dried variety, which have an intense woody, musky scent that works beautifully with cream sauces, Madeira, and white meats. With fresh morels, a lighter preparation is better, so I like to stew them gently in good butter with some diced celery root and tomato.

Trim and wash the mushrooms, then leave them on a cloth to drain thoroughly.

Peel and dice the celery root and blanch it in boiling salted water for a few seconds. Refresh in iced water, then drain and place with the morels.

Heat a tablespoon of butter in a pan over low heat and sweat the shallots until tender. Add the morels and celery root, then turn up the heat a little and cook until the mushrooms have softened, 4–5 minutes. Add the lemon juice, the rest of the butter, and seasoning. Just before serving, add the diced tomato and a few basil leaves.

SERVES 4

7 oz fresh morels
4 oz celery root
2 tbsp unsalted butter
2 shallots, peeled and
    chopped
juice of 1 lemon
1 large plum tomato,
    blanched, skinned,
    and diced
basil leaves
salt
black pepper

Salade d'asperges

ASPARAGUS SALAD

Seeing the first asparagus in the market is a joy and means that spring is most definitely with us. The white variety favored by those in northeastern Europe, including Alsace, is delicious, but in my view not as flavorsome and versatile as the luscious green or purple variety. Here are three of my favorite sauces to go with asparagus. Always serve warm or at room temperature but never cold, as this blunts the taste.

Take the asparagus and bend the stalk of each one until it snaps, then discard these woody ends. Peel the stalks using a peeler.

Tie the asparagus in bundles and cook in boiling salted water until tender, then refresh in iced water to stop the cooking and retain the color. Drain well and serve with your chosen dressing or sauce.

VINAIGRETTE AUX HERBES ET OEUF DUR

Mix the oil, vinegar, mustard, and seasoning, then fold in the herbs and chopped eggs.

SAUCE MALTAISE

Blanch the orange peel in plenty of boiling water for 1 minute, then drain. Chop finely, then put it in a small pan with the juice and sugar and boil until syrupy. Let cool a little, then add to the hollandaise.

CRÈME FOUETTÉE À LA TRUFFE

Whisk the cream into soft peaks. Add the crème fraîche, lemon juice, and seasoning, then the grated truffle.

SERVES 4

2½ lb asparagus
   (untrimmed weight)
salt

VINAIGRETTE AUX HERBES
   ET OEUF DUR

¼ cup extra-virgin olive oil
1 tbsp red wine vinegar
1 tbsp Dijon mustard
2 tbsp mixed snipped fresh
   herbs (tarragon, parsley,
   chives, chervil)
2 free-range eggs, hard-
   boiled and chopped
salt
black pepper

SAUCE MALTAISE

thinly pared peel of 1 orange
juice of 3 oranges
1½ tbsp brown sugar
⅔ cup hollandaise sauce
   (see page 330)

CRÈME FOUETTÉE À LA
   TRUFFE (TRUFFLE
   DRESSING)

⅔ cup whipping cream
1 tbsp crème fraîche
juice of 1 lemon
6 tbsp truffle, grated
   (canned are fine)

Bombine Ardèchoise

POTATOES AND PORCINI, ARDÈCHE STYLE

This is a traditional dish in the Ardèche region of
France and there are as many versions as villages!
Every family has its own recipe, but this is my favorite.
Delicious on its own, or a perfect accompaniment
to a roast chicken.

If using fresh porcini, wipe them clean, then slice. If using dried porcini,
soak them in cold water until soft and reconstituted.

Boil the potatoes in salted water until tender, then drain, peel, and slice.
Blanch the snow peas in boiling water, then plunge them into iced water to
stop the cooking and keep their color. Cook the green beans in the same way.

Heat the duck fat or oil in a heavy-bottomed frying pan until smoking hot.
Add the sliced potatoes and fry, turning them frequently, until beautifully
golden brown all over. Turn down the heat, add the porcini, shallots, snow
peas, and green beans, then season with salt and black pepper. Cook for
2 minutes, add the garlic and parsley, then mix and serve immediately.

SERVES 4

7 oz fresh porcini or
   2 oz dried porcini
16 new potatoes
5 oz snow peas, trimmed
4 oz haricots verts (French
   green beans), trimmed
3 tbsp duck fat or olive oil
2 shallots, peeled and
   chopped
2 garlic cloves, peeled and
   finely chopped
1 tbsp chopped curly parsley
salt
black pepper

Salade bagatelle

CARROT AND ASPARAGUS SALAD

This colorful salad combines the lovely sweetness of young carrots with a sharp peppery kick from watercress. It is a classic, usually served as an accompaniment to a main course.

Mix the ingredients for the dressing together and set aside.

Take the asparagus and bend the stalk of each one until it snaps, then discard these woody ends. Peel the stems with a peeler. Peel the carrots.

Tie the asparagus in bundles and cook them in boiling salted water until tender, then refresh in iced water to stop the cooking and retain the color. Drain well and cut on an angle into ¼-inch slices. Boil the carrots until tender, then refresh and slice.

Toss the carrot and asparagus with dressing to taste, then finish with a little watercress also dipped in the dressing. Just before serving, sprinkle the sliced mushrooms on top.

SERVES 4

DRESSING
½ tbsp Dijon mustard
1 tbsp white wine vinegar
4 tbsp olive oil
salt
black pepper

2 bunches large green
  asparagus
4 new-season carrots
2 bunches watercress,
  spun dry
12 white mushrooms,
  wiped and sliced

La salade Aveyronnaise

WARM SALAD WITH SWEETBREADS AND ROQUEFORT

L'Aveyron in the Midi-Pyrénées is where one of the greatest of all blue cheeses is made – Roquefort. This pungent, salty, creamy ewe's milk cheese is shown off to good effect in this delicious warm salad.

Trim and spin dry the salad leaves.

To blanch the sweetbreads, put them in a pan of salted water, bring to a boil, and cook for 6 minutes. Drain and rinse under cold water. Peel the membrane off the sweetbreads, then roll them in the seasoned flour. Heat 1 tablespoon of the oil with the butter in a frying pan, add the sweetbreads, and fry until brown and crispy.

Warm the crème fraîche in a pan, then whisk in the Roquefort until it melts. Season with a little salt and pepper.

Add the thinly sliced shallot to the salad leaves and toss with the lemon juice, remaining oil, and salt and pepper. Spoon some Roquefort cream onto each plate and add the warm sweetbreads and salad on top. Serve at once.

SERVES 4

8 oz mâche

4 oz escarole or curly endive

6 oz lamb sweetbreads

all-purpose flour, seasoned
    with salt and pepper

3 tbsp vegetable oil

1 tbsp unsalted butter

3 tbsp crème fraîche

3 oz Roquefort cheese

1 shallot, peeled and thinly
    sliced

juice of ½ lemon

salt

black pepper

Salade caprice de reine

ENDIVE, APPLE, AND TRUFFLE SALAD

When Le Gavroche and the Waterside Inn first opened, salads were always offered as side dishes with all main courses, never as a starter. On some of the earlier menus *salade du jour* also featured and most were as elaborate as this recipe.

Cut the endives into manageable bite-sized strips. Remove the leaves from the celery and set them aside for garnishing the salad, then cut the celery heart into strips about the same size as the endive. Put the endive and celery in iced water for 20 minutes to firm up, then drain well.

Peel the apples and cut them into matchsticks, then put them into a little water and lemon juice to keep them white.

Mix the mayonnaise with the crème fraîche in a serving bowl and season with salt and pepper and the remaining lemon juice.

Put the endive, celery, and apple sticks in a bowl and garnish with thin shavings of truffle. Serve with the mayonnaise and crème fraîche sauce to spoon over.

SERVES 6

7 oz Belgian endives

1 head celery, tender heart only

3 eating apples (such as Golden Delicious)

juice of 1 lemon

2 tbsp mayonnaise (see page 332)

2 tbsp crème fraîche

6 tbsp fresh or cooked truffles

salt

black pepper

Salade de betterave aux noix

BEET AND WALNUT SALAD

There are many varieties of beets in different colors, but the best ones for this recipe are the long, carrot-shaped *"crapaudine"* variety, which has a superior flavor, and the beautiful stripy Chioggia beets. If you cannot find these particular types, use large, normal red beets. I prefer to bake beets, especially for salads, as this intensifies their taste and natural sweetness.

Preheat the oven to 400°F. Bake the washed beets as you would bake a potato – this should take about 30–40 minutes.

Meanwhile, if you have time, skin the walnuts by soaking them in a little boiling milk, then peeling them with the point of a small knife. This is a fiddly job but worth the effort, as the skin can leave a bitter tannic taste. Mix the mustard, red wine vinegar, and walnut oil to make the dressing and season with salt and pepper.

When the beets are cool enough to handle, peel them, cut them into a mixture of cubes and thin slices, and douse them with some of the dressing while still lukewarm – beets soak up dressing better if not fridge cold.

Fold in the sliced shallots, parsley, and a little more dressing if necessary just before serving, then garnish with the walnuts.

SERVES 4

4 large beets
16 walnut kernels
milk
½ tbsp Dijon mustard
1 tbsp red wine vinegar
4 tbsp walnut oil
2 shallots, peeled and finely
    sliced
1 tbsp coarsely chopped
    flat-leaf parsley
salt
black pepper

Salade pomone

FRISÉE, APPLE, AND GRUYÈRE SALAD

I'm not sure of the orgins of this salad, but it is one of
my favorites. The combination of bitter salad leaves,
crunchy tart apple, sweet spicy mustard, and savory
cheese is divine. Savora mustard is an aromatic
mustard that's popular in the north of France.

SERVES 4

1 head frisée lettuce
4 russet apples
1 lemon
4 tbsp olive oil
1 tbsp white wine vinegar
½ tbsp Savora mustard
4 oz Gruyère cheese, grated
1 tbsp snipped chives
salt
black pepper

Pick through the frisée, then carefully wash and drain the leaves. Peel the
apples and cut them into ¼-inch dice. Put these in a bowl of water with a
squeeze of lemon to keep them white.

To make the dressing, mix the oil, vinegar, mustard, and salt and pepper.
Toss the salad leaves with the apple, grated cheese, and dressing, then
sprinkle the snipped chives on top.

*Les animaux se repaissent,
l'homme mange; l'homme d'esprit
seul sait manger*

Beasts feed, man eats; only man,
with his intellect, knows how to eat
JEAN ANTHELME BRILLAT-SAVARIN

Gratin de cardons

BAKED CARDOON AND BONE MARROW

The cardoon belongs to the artichoke and thistle family and grows wild in the Mediterranean region, where it has been eaten since Greek and Roman times. It's still a popular vegetable in parts of France – my wife's family always grows cardoon and serves it stewed with tomato sauce. This particular recipe is a Lyonnaise speciality, and can be served as a starter, an accompaniment, or even as a main dish. Choose a cardoon that feels heavy, and discard the first layer of stalks, which tend to be stringy and hollow.

SERVES 6

1 cardoon

1 tbsp all-purpose flour

juice of 1 lemon

2 oz Gruyère cheese, grated

3 tbsp beef jus
(see page 328)

2 tbsp cooked truffle,
thinly sliced

4 oz veal bone marrow,
cut into ¼-inch slices

1 tbsp unsalted butter,
for greasing dishes

salt

black pepper

Peel the stalks of the cardoon as you would celery, removing the strings and any discolored parts. Cut into manageable pieces about 6 inches in length and put them in a saucepan. Add cold water, running it through a fine sieve containing the flour. This makes what is called a *blanc* in French culinary parlance and helps to keep the cardoon white. Add the lemon juice and a little salt.

Bring the water to a boil, then cover with a piece of parchment paper and simmer for about an hour until the cardoon is tender. Drain and cut the cardoon into bite-sized diamond shapes.

Preheat the oven to 425°F. Arrange a neat layer of cardoon on the bases of individual heatproof dishes or in one large dish. Sprinkle with a little Gruyère layer followed by some beef jus, then repeat the layers twice more. Finish with some slices of truffle and bone marrow, then top with the rest of the Gruyère. Place in the hot oven for 6–7 minutes, then finish under the broiler for a lovely brown top.

Salade jardinière

GARDEN SALAD

This is a deliciously light, summery salad that's just right for lunch in the garden or to freshen the palate after a meaty main course.

Prepare the vegetables. Peel the turnip and carrot and cut into ⅛-inch-thick batons, and trim the beans and cauliflower florets. Bend the stalk of each asparagus spear until it snaps, then discard these woody ends and peel the stalks.

To make the vinaigrette, whisk all the ingredients together. You'll have more than you need for this recipe, but the dressing keeps well in an airtight jar and can be used for other salads.

Cook the vegetables separately in boiling salted water until al dente, then refresh them in iced water. Drain and dry well, then dress with the vinaigrette. Finish with a sprinkle of chervil and tarragon leaves.

SERVES 4

2 medium-sized white
    turnips
1 large carrot
2 oz haricots verts (French
    green beans)
4 oz cauliflower florets
1 bunch asparagus
½ cup shelled peas
chopped fresh chervil *and*
    tarragon

VINAIGRETTE

2 tbsp olive oil
6 tbsp vegetable oil
2 tsp Dijon mustard
2 tbsp white wine vinegar
salt
black pepper

Tarte tatin de légumes

ROAST VEGETABLE TART

This is a wonderful stand-alone starter or main course
and also makes a good accompaniment to a plain roast.
Apple *tarte Tatin* is a classic dessert, but this sweet-
and-savory take on the original is just as enjoyable. It
can be made in a suitably sized ovenproof frying pan,
or in individual pans if you prefer. Vary the vegetables
according to your taste and what's in season.

Preheat the oven to 425°F. Cut the vegetables into 1¼- to 1½-inch pieces
and spread them on a baking sheet. Season and drizzle them with olive oil,
then roast in the hot oven for 8–10 minutes. The vegetables should be partly
cooked and have a little color. Leave the oven on.

Melt the butter in an ovenproof pan, then sprinkle on the sugar. Put the
cooked vegetables, sliced chile (seeded if you like), and thyme leaves on top,
making sure to pack the vegetables tightly.

Roll out the pastry to about ⅛ inch thick and place it over the vegetables,
taking care to tuck it under them around the edges. Make a few holes in
the pastry with the point of a knife, then bake the tart in the oven – still at
425°F – for 20 minutes. Leave the tart to cool a little before turning it out
and serving.

SERVES 4

2 Belgian endives, trimmed
1 carrot, peeled
1 small parsnip, peeled
1 medium turnip, peeled
1 large onion, peeled
2 tbsp olive oil
2 tbsp unsalted butter
2 tbsp superfine sugar
1 red chile, sliced
leaves from 1 sprig of thyme
7 oz all-butter puff pastry
salt
black pepper

Salade tiède de choux au canard fumé

WARM CABBAGE SALAD WITH SMOKED DUCK

A pointed spring cabbage or a napa cabbage is good for
this salad, or even sliced large Brussels sprouts. Serve
as an accompaniment to duck confit or as a starter,
perhaps with a fried duck egg perched on top.

SERVES 4

1 smoked duck breast
2 tbsp duck fat
1 pointed spring cabbage
  (about 12 oz)
1 shallot, peeled but left
  whole
1 garlic clove, peeled
1½ tbsp red wine vinegar
salt
black pepper

Remove the fat from the smoked duck, chop it up, and place it in a pan with
a tablespoon of the duck fat. Cook over medium heat until the pieces have
rendered their fat and are crispy, like pork cracklings, about 30 minutes.
Remove, leaving the melted fat in the pan, and keep warm.

Slice the cabbage and shallot very thinly and mash the garlic to a paste. Add
the remaining duck fat to the pan and fry the cabbage, shallot, and garlic
over medium-high heat. You want the cabbage to take on a little color, but
keep it slightly underdone. Season, add the thinly sliced smoked duck breast
and the pieces of crispy fat, then finish with the vinegar.

If serving with an egg, fry it in a little duck fat to make the dish even more
ducky and indulgent.

Riz à la Valencienne

RICE WITH HAM, MUSHROOMS, AND ARTICHOKES

This versatile rice dish can be eaten as a starter or as
an accompaniment to poultry or sausages. It can even
be chilled, then drizzled with a little vinaigrette and
served as a summer salad. Either way it's a delicious
combination of tastes. You can use the preserved
artichokes sold in good Italian delis.

Cook the mushrooms over medium heat in ½ tablespoon of the butter and a
little lemon juice until tender. Drain them, then slice and set aside. Add the
cooking liquid to the chicken stock.

Preheat the oven to 400°F. Melt a tablespoon of butter in an ovenproof
pan and sweat the chopped onion over low heat until soft and lightly colored.
Add the rice, stir well, then add the diced ham and the stock. Bring to a
boil, then cover with a piece of parchment paper and place in the oven for
25 minutes. Remove and let rest for 5 minutes. The rice should have
absorbed all the liquid.

Add the sliced artichokes, cooked mushrooms, and remaining butter to
the rice. Season with a little paprika and salt and pepper and fluff up with
a fork before serving.

SERVES 4

12 small mushrooms, wiped
2 tbsp unsalted butter
juice of 1 lemon
2 cups chicken stock
    (see page 320)
1 large onion, peeled and
    chopped
1 cup long-grain rice
2 oz cured ham, diced
4 baby artichokes, cooked
    and sliced
paprika
salt
black pepper

Orge perlé façon risotto

BARLEY RISOTTO

Lots of grains can be cooked like a risotto and make
a change from rice. This version makes a perfect
accompaniment to game dishes that are served with lots
of sauce. The ground almonds add a touch of sweetness.

Drain the barley. Melt a tablespoon of the butter in a pan over low heat
and sweat the finely chopped onion until translucent. Add the barley and
continue to cook for 4–5 minutes, then add the picked thyme leaves and the
wine. When the liquid has almost evaporated, add enough of the hot stock
to cover and continue to simmer gently.

Cook as a rice risotto, adding more hot stock a little at a time and stirring
frequently. The barley should absorb all the stock and you might need to
add a little more heated liquid, depending on how dry it is.

After about 30 minutes of gentle cooking, the barley should be tender so take
the pan off the heat and fold in the ground almonds, Parmesan, remaining
butter, and seasoning.

SERVES 6

1 cup pearl barley, soaked
  in water for 2 hours
2 tbsp unsalted butter
1 onion, peeled and finely
  chopped
1 sprig of thyme, leaves
  picked
$\frac{1}{2}$ cup dry white wine
$2\frac{1}{2}$ cups chicken stock
  (see page 320), or as
  needed, heated
$\frac{1}{2}$ cup ground almonds
2 oz Parmesan cheese,
  grated
salt
black pepper

Sweet things are a treat and can be enjoyed at any time – not only at the end of a meal. They are an unnecessary indulgence but should bring pleasure and a smile. Pâtisserie does not have to be complex to be good, although some of the more elaborate recipes will be sure to impress, but a good pastry, lovingly prepared from great ingredients, will always be welcome at any table. France does have its regional specialities in desserts as in other dishes, but common to all regions is the use of local and seasonal produce.

Desserts

Tarte aux poires Bourdaloue

PEAR AND ALMOND TART

Probably my favorite fruit tart, this is simply
irresistible – especially when served warm. The name
may come from a street in Paris, rue Bourdaloue, where
there was a famous pâtisserie, and the street, in turn,
was named after Louis Bourdaloue, a seventeenth-
century French Jesuit. Whatever the origins of its title,
this confection of poached pears, almond cream, and
crisp pastry is an absolute delight.

Peel the pears, cut them in half, and remove the cores. Pour about 1¼ cups
water into a large pan and add the vanilla pod, cinnamon stick, and 1 cup
sugar. Bring to a boil, then add the pears and simmer them for 20 minutes.
Let cool. You can do all this the day before making the tart if you like.

To make the pastry, cut the butter into small pieces and leave it to soften at
room temperature. Sift the flour and salt, place them on the work surface,
and make a well in the center. Add the butter and 2 tbsp sugar and gently
work together with your fingertips. Add the egg yolk and gradually draw
in the flour, adding drops of water as you go. When all the flour has been
incorporated, shape the dough into a ball, but do not overwork it. Wrap
the pastry in plastic wrap and refrigerate for at least 2 hours before using.

For the almond cream, whisk the butter and ½ cup sugar until pale, then add
the ground almonds. Whisk in the eggs, one at a time, and finally the rum.

Preheat the oven to 400°F. Roll out the pastry on a floured surface to a
thickness of about ⅛ inch and use it to line a greased 11-inch flan pan.
Prick the pastry base with a fork, line it with parchment paper, and fill with
baking beans, then bake blind for 20 minutes. Remove the paper and beans
and put the pastry back into the oven until the base has cooked but not taken
on too much color, another 5 minutes. Leave the oven on.

Spoon the almond cream into the tart base, then arrange the sliced,
drained pears on top, with the pointed ends towards the center. Bake
in the preheated oven for 40 minutes.

When the tart is cooked, warm some apricot jam with a little water and
brush it over the surface. Sprinkle the tart with toasted sliced almonds
and serve warm.

SERVES 8

POACHED PEARS

4 pears (Williams are good)
1 vanilla pod, split
1 cinnamon stick
1 cup superfine sugar

SWEET PASTRY

5 tbsp unsalted butter
1 cup (4½ oz) all-purpose
    flour, plus extra
    for dusting
pinch salt
2 tbsp granulated sugar
1 free-range egg yolk
1 tbsp water

ALMOND CREAM

½ cup softened unsalted
    butter
½ cup superfine sugar
1 cup ground almonds
3 medium free-range eggs
2 tbsp rum

TO FINISH

apricot jam warmed with
    a little water
1 tbsp sliced almonds,
    toasted

Beignets à la crème

CREAM FRITTERS

Everyone likes fritters or doughnuts once in a while, and these are a real sweet temptation. They are rich, though, so best for occasional consumption only. The fruit tempers the richness well and can be varied according to the season and your preference.

First make the cream filling. Whisk the sugar, egg, and egg yolks together in a bowl, then whisk in the flour. Bring the milk to a boil in a pan with the strips of peel and pour this onto the egg mixture. Whisk well, then pour everything back into the pan and heat until boiling. It will become very thick, so keep whisking to prevent the mixture from sticking or burning. Line a shallow baking sheet measuring about 12 x 8 inches with plastic wrap. Remove the orange peel from the mixture and spread it out on the lined sheet. Cover and chill for until set, 2–3 hours.

To make the raspberry coulis for the garnish, blitz the raspberries with the 1/2 cup sugar and lemon juice to taste. Pass through a fine sieve.

Cut the sticks of rhubarb into pieces about 1½ inches long. Melt the ⅓ cup superfine sugar in the grenadine – you may need to add a tablespoon of water. Place the rhubarb pieces in a wide pan so that they fit snugly, and add the liquid. Simmer for 2–3 minutes, then carefully flip them over. Make sure not to overcook the rhubarb – it should retain a little bite.

Make the batter at the last moment by mixing the dry ingredients in a bowl, then whisking in the water. Pour the oil into a large pan or a deep-fat fryer and heat to 350°F.

Take a spoonful of the cream mixture and dip it into the batter, then carefully place it into the hot frying oil. Cook just a few beignets at a time, moving them around in the oil with a slotted spoon, until golden and crisp, 30 seconds–1 minute. Take care not to overcrowd the pan.

Drain the beignets on paper towels and serve them warm with the raspberry coulis and poached rhubarb. Sprinkle with a little confectioners' sugar before serving.

SERVES 6

CREAM FILLING
¼ cup superfine sugar
1 free-range egg
4 free-range egg yolks
⅔ cup (3 oz) all-purpose
  flour
2 cups milk
thinly pared peel of
  2 oranges, cut into
  fine strips

GARNISH
14 oz raspberries
½ cup sugar
juice of ½ lemon
4 sticks of rhubarb
⅓ cup superfine sugar
1 tbsp grenadine syrup

BATTER
½ cup cornstarch
1½ cups (6½ oz) all-purpose
  flour
1 tsp baking powder
2 cups carbonated water
2 quarts vegetable oil,
  for deep-frying

1 tsp confectioners' sugar,
  for serving

Panna cotta au babeurre et figues

BUTTERMILK PANNA COTTA WITH FIGS

This is a very lightly set panna cotta that can't be turned out, so make it in pretty glass bowls for serving. The panna cottas are topped with pistachio crumbs made from a shortbread-like mixture and decorated with tuiles and figs. Make all the trimmings to create a really special dessert, or just garnish with figs – up to you. It will always be a delight.

To make the panna cottas, pour the cream into a pan and add the fig leaves, vanilla pods, and sugar. Bring this to a boil, then whisk in the gelatin and pour in the buttermilk. Stir, then strain through a sieve into 12 glass bowls and leave in the fridge to set for 8 hours.

For the tuiles, heat all the ingredients except the baking soda in a pan to 284°F, or until the mixture starts to turn golden. Stir in the baking soda, then pour the mixture into a deep dish lined with a silicone baking mat or parchment paper. Be very careful, as it will spit and splash. Leave this to cool and set.

Preheat the oven to 400°F. Blitz the cooled honeycomb to a powder in a food processor, then sprinkle it onto a silicone baking mat or a baking sheet lined with parchment paper and put it in the oven for a couple of minutes until melted. Cut into whatever shapes you like.

For the pistachio crumbs, mix the flour, ground almonds, and sugar together. Using your fingertips, gently work in the butter and pistachios – the mixture should just come together into a paste, so don't overwork it. Wrap it in plastic wrap and chill for an hour.

Preheat the oven to 350°F. Roll out the pistachio paste to about ¼–⅜ inch thick and place it on a baking sheet. Prick it with a fork and cook for about 25 minutes. Let cool, then break up into crumbs.

Toss the figs in the oil and pepper, then cut into bite-sized pieces.

When the panna cottas are set, serve them topped with pistachio crumbs and a couple of tuiles and figs.

SERVES 12

PANNA COTTA

2 cups heavy cream
4 fig leaves
2 vanilla pods, split
⅞ cup superfine sugar
4 leaves gelatin (softened in cold water and squeezed)
2 cups buttermilk

HONEYCOMB TUILES

⅔ cup superfine sugar
1 tbsp honey
¼ cup liquid glucose
2 tbsp water
1¾ tsp baking soda

PISTACHIO CRUMBS

½ cup (2 oz) all-purpose flour
¼ cup ground almonds
¼ cup superfine sugar
2 generous tbsp unsalted butter, melted
¼ cup pistachio nuts, finely chopped

DRESSED FIGS

4 figs, cut into quarters
1 tbsp extra-virgin olive oil
black pepper

Babas au Calvados

CALVADOS BABAS

One of the many great things about this recipe is that nearly all the work can be done well in advance, leaving just the final glaze and assembly when you're ready to eat. The traditional baba is served with rum and I remember as an apprentice not being allowed to make these delicious cakes for fear that I would get inebriated. This version uses Calvados, another potent spirit, and is just as good. If serving kids, leave the Calvados out of the syrup and let the adults help themselves. You can make babas in any shape, such as rings, but I like to use little molds of about 1½ by 1½ inches.

Dissolve the yeast in the milk in a stand mixer bowl. Add the flour, honey, salt, and eggs and knead with the dough hook attachment for 5 minutes. Scrape down the edges, add the butter, and continue to work the dough until the butter has been incorporated. Cover and let rise for 45 minutes.

Preheat the oven to 400°F. Butter your molds, unless they are nonstick silicone ones. Punch down the dough, then half-fill the baba molds with it. Leave them to rise again for 30 minutes, then bake in the preheated oven until golden and fully cooked – this should take about 20 minutes. Take the babas out of the molds and let cool on a rack.

To make the compote, peel and roughly chop the apples. Put them in a pan with the sugar and a splash of water, then bring to a simmer. Mash the apples as they cook until you have a soft compote. Let cool until needed.

To make the syrup, put the lemongrass in a small pan with the apple juice, lime juice, and sugar. Bring to a boil and then pass through a fine sieve. Add Calvados to taste. Dunk the babas in the lukewarm syrup until swollen, plump, and completely soaked. The syrup shouldn't be too hot, or the babas may crack, but if it is too cold, the babas will not soak as well. Place them on a wire rack to drain, then refrigerate until needed.

Just before serving, make the glaze. Pour the apple juice into a pan, add the sugar, and boil until the sugar has melted. Mix the cornstarch and lemon juice, then whisk this into the boiling apple juice to thicken. Brush the babas with the glaze to give them a lovely sheen, then serve on a bed of apple compote. Top with Chantilly cream and apple crisps if you like.

MAKES 8 BABAS

¼ oz (8 g) fresh yeast
2 tbsp warm milk (110–115°F)
1⅔ cups (7 oz) all-purpose flour
2 tsp clear honey
2 tsp salt
3 medium free-range eggs
5 tbsp softened, unsalted butter, plus extra for greasing

APPLE COMPOTE

4 eating apples (Braeburns or Pippins)
4 tbsp sugar

SYRUP

2 stalks lemongrass, tough outer layer peeled away and interior roughly chopped
1 cup pure apple juice
juice of 2 limes
½ cup brown sugar
good splash of Calvados

GLAZE

1 cup fresh (cloudy) apple juice
5 tsp superfine sugar
2½ tbsp cornstarch
2 tbsp lemon juice

Chantilly cream, for serving (see page 340)
apple crisps, for serving (see page 338)

Marquise au chocolat

CHOCOLATE MARQUISE

This almost-forgotten French classic is a wonderful
layered construction of biscuit and flavored ganache.
It's perfect for a special occasion, as you can make
it in advance and keep it in the fridge ready to slice
when you want. There are many variations, but this
recipe, with the retro touch of After Eight mints, was
on the menu at Le Gavroche back in the early days and
is just as popular when it makes an appearance now.
The quantities here make a little more biscuit than
you need to allow for trimmings and any mishaps – no
hardship to finish them up though.

First make the biscuit. Preheat the oven to 400°F. Line a baking sheet with
lightly buttered and floured parchment paper. Whisk the egg whites until
frothy, then add 1 cup of the sugar and continue to whisk until firm. Fold in
the ground almonds, remaining sugar, and milk powder. Spread the mixture
onto the lined baking sheet to a thickness of ¼ inch and sprinkle with the
hazelnuts. Cook in the preheated oven until just set, 20 minutes. Let cool,
then cut into 3 neat strips measuring 8 x 3½ inches.

Next, make the ganache. Melt the chocolate in a bowl over barely simmering
water – don't let it get too hot. Whip the cream to soft peaks. Pour half the
melted chocolate onto the cream and mix with a whisk, then gently add
the remaining chocolate. Divide this into 3 portions and flavor one with
rum, one with crème de menthe, and leave the third plain. Leave until cool
and semi-set to the consistency of thick mayonnaise – it needs to be firm
enough to build your marquise.

Cut a piece of card measuring 8 x 3½ inches and cover it with foil – this will
be your base for the marquise. Place a strip of biscuit on the base, spread
it with a layer of rum ganache, then sprinkle on the chopped ginger. Add
another strip of biscuit, spread with the crème de menthe ganache, and
arrange the After Eights on top. Add the third biscuit, then spread the plain
ganache over the top and sides and smooth with a palette knife. Place the
marquise in the fridge to set for at least an hour.

When you're ready to serve, dip a knife in hot water and cut the marquise
into slices about ¾ inch thick.

SERVES 12

BISCUIT
butter, for greasing
all-purpose flour, for dusting
5 free-range egg whites
1 cup plus 2½ tbsp superfine
    sugar
⅔ cup ground almonds
2 tbsp milk powder
2 tbsp chopped hazelnuts

GANACHE
1½ lb extra bitter chocolate
3 cups heavy cream
2 tbsp dark rum
2 tsbp crème de menthe
2 oz crystallized ginger,
    coarsely chopped
18 After Eight mints

Feuilleté aux raisins et Kirsch

PUFF PASTRY WITH GRAPES AND KIRSCH

This is an impressive-looking dessert, but can be made with store-bought puff pastry and most of the work can be done in advance. The light, crisp *feuilletés* – puff pastry rounds – are slightly hollowed out, which makes them lighter, and filled with mouthwateringly good Kirsch-soaked grapes. The longer these are soaked, the better they are. Put it all together with the warm sabayon sauce at the last minute and serve right away.

SERVES 4

confectioners' sugar,
    for dusting
12 oz all-butter puff pastry
11 oz seedless white grapes
7 tbsp Kirsch
½ cup superfine sugar
6 medium free-range
    egg yolks

Dust your work surface with confectioners' sugar and roll out the pastry to a thickness of ¼ inch. Cut out 8 rounds and place these on a moistened nonstick baking sheet – brushing the baking sheet with water stops the pastry from shrinking. Leave the pastry to rest in the fridge for at least 20 minutes.

Meanwhile, peel the grapes with a small knife or a teaspoon, and put them in the Kirsch to marinate. Make a sugar syrup by boiling the superfine sugar with the 5 tablespoons water. Preheat the oven to 450°F.

Dust the puff pastry rounds with a little more confectioners' sugar and put them in the preheated oven for 5 minutes. Turn the heat down to 350°F and cook until golden brown and puffed up, another 10 minutes. Place on a wire rack to cool.

Drain the grapes, reserving the Kirsch. Put them in a pan with half the sugar syrup and warm through over low heat.

To make the sabayon, put the egg yolks, Kirsch (collected from the grapes), and the rest of the sugar syrup in a bowl over a pan of simmering water. Whisk over low heat until you have a smooth, rich sauce and the whisk leaves a trail when lifted.

Using the point of a knife, carefully hollow out the pastry rounds – working from the top of 4 of them and from the bottom of the other 4 – removing any pastry that may not have fully cooked. Place the 4 bases on a plate, fill with the warmed grapes and sabayon, and pop the lids on top. Serve at once.

Kouign-amann

LAYERED BUTTER YEAST CAKE

A true Brittany classic, this yeast cake has many variations, but all are laden with local butter. The name comes from the local dialect – *kouign,* meaning cake and *amann,* meaning butter. This is at its best when freshly baked and needs nothing more than a cup of milky coffee or a glass of local sweet cider.

SERVES 8

½ oz (15 g) fresh yeast
¾ cup warm water
    (110–115°F)
2⅓ cup (9½ oz) all-purpose
    flour, plus extra
    for dusting
pinch sea salt
7 tbsp salted butter
⅞ cup superfine sugar

Dissolve the yeast in the water, add the flour and salt, then begin to knead until you have a smooth dough. It may seem a little sticky, but that's fine. Cover the dough and leave it to rise for an hour.

Roll the dough out on a floured surface to make a rectangle about 12 inches long and 8 inches wide. Cut the butter into ¾-inch cubes and scatter them down the middle of the rectangle with 3 tablespoons of the sugar. Fold the pastry over, sprinkle on another 3 tablespoons sugar, then fold again to form what is almost a square.

Wrap the dough in plastic wrap and refrigerate for 45 minutes. Repeat the rolling process, adding another 3 tablespoons sugar at each fold. Leave the dough to rest for 30 minutes, then roll it out into a 8-inch circle and place it in a flan or pie dish.

Let rise again for 30 minutes, then sprinkle over a little more sugar and a couple of extra knobs of salted butter if feeling particularly indulgent. Preheat the oven to 425°F.

Place the dish in the hot oven for 20 minutes, then turn the temperature down to 400°F for a further 20 minutes. Eat the cake while it is still warm.

Tarte Bressane

SUGAR TART

Also known as *tarte au sucre,* this is a delicious yeasty brioche-like tart covered in cream and sugar from the Bresse region of France (north of Lyon). There are many variations, including some with pink pralines, but this is the one that I like the most. Delicious on its own or with some fruit compote, and best served warm.

Dissolve the yeast in the milk in the bowl of a stand mixer. Add the flour, sugar, salt, and eggs and knead with the dough hook attachment until you have an elastic dough. Add the melted butter and continue to work for at least 5 minutes, scraping down the mixture from the edges when necessary. Cover and let rise for 1 hour. Lightly butter an 8-inch flan dish.

Punch down the dough to release the gases, then transfer it to the flan dish. Spread the dough out, then cover with plastic wrap and let rise again – this time for just 20 minutes. Preheat the oven to 425°F.

Place the tart in the preheated oven for 10 minutes. Split the vanilla pod and scrape out the seeds, then mix them into the crème fraîche. Take the tart out of the oven and spread the crème fraîche over the top. Quickly sprinkle on the brown sugar and return the tart to the oven until fully cooked and brown on top, a further 20 minutes.

SERVES 6

1/3 oz (10 g) fresh yeast

2 tsp warm milk (110–115°F)

2 cups (8½ oz) all-purpose flour

¼ cup superfine sugar

1 tsp salt

3 medium free-range eggs

5 tbsp unsalted butter, melted, plus extra for greasing

TOPPING

1 vanilla pod

6 oz crème fraîche

1/3 cup brown sugar

Coupe de pêche rose chéri

PEACHES WITH CHERRIES AND CREAM

Best served in fancy glasses with some wafers or crisp cookies, this luscious peach confection is as old as the famous peach Melba, but is flavored with cherries instead of raspberries.

Bring a pan of water to a boil, add the peaches, and blanch them for a couple of minutes. Refresh them in iced water, then peel off the skins.

Make a sugar syrup by boiling $2\frac{2}{3}$ cups of the superfine sugar with 1 quart water for 5 minutes. Carefully add the peaches to the boiling syrup and simmer for 20 minutes, then let cool.

Put the cherries in a wide saucepan with the remaining $\frac{2}{3}$ cups superfine sugar and the lemon juice and bring to a boil. Add the red currant jelly and continue to cook until the jelly has melted, then let cool.

Whisk the cream with the confectioners' sugar until stiff. Spoon some cherries and their sauce into each glass. Cut the peaches in half, remove the pits, and fill the cavities with ice cream. Place the peaches on top of the cherries and pipe the whipped cream on top.

SERVES 6

6 yellow peaches
$3\frac{1}{3}$ cups superfine sugar
10 oz dark cherries, pitted
juice of 1 lemon
$\frac{1}{2}$ cup red currant jelly
1 cup whipping cream,
   whipped
$\frac{3}{4}$ cup confectioners' sugar
vanilla ice cream

Soufflé aux fraises

STRAWBERRY CRUMBLE SOUFFLÉ

Strawberries go beautifully with Kirsch, and these little soufflés are gorgeous. Make them in individual ramekins of about 3 by 2½ inches and serve them with some clotted cream if you like.

Wash and hull the strawberries, then place them in a pan with the demerara sugar, lemon juice, and 2 tablespoons water. Bring to a simmer, stir gently, and cook until tender. Remove 1 or 2 strawberries per person to serve as a garnish and douse them with the Kirsch.

Put the rest of the strawberries in a food processor with the cooking juices and blitz them to a purée. Pass the purée through a fine sieve into a clean saucepan. Mix the cornstarch with 2 tablespoons water to make a paste and add this to the purée. Bring to a boil, stirring constantly to avoid any lumps. Leave the mixture to cool, but do not refrigerate.

To make the crumble topping, mix all the ingredients together and spread the mixture over a nonstick baking sheet. Preheat the oven to 425°F. Toast the crumble for a few minutes, then remove and turn the oven down to 400°F.

Whisk the egg whites until frothy, then add the ⅓ cup superfine sugar and continue to whisk until stiff peaks form. Take a third of the egg whites and beat them into the cooled purée, then gently fold in the rest of the egg whites. Butter your ramekins thoroughly and coat the insides with sugar. Always work upwards when buttering soufflé dishes, as this helps the soufflés rise.

Half-fill the ramekins with the strawberry mixture, then add the reserved strawberries and Kirsch. Fill the ramekins to the top, level with a palette knife, and place them in the preheated oven for 8 minutes. Sprinkle on some crumble topping and continue to cook for a further 2–3 minutes. Serve with a spoonful of clotted cream if you like.

SERVES 8

21 oz strawberries
4 tbsp demerara sugar
juice of 1 lemon
2 tbsp Kirsch
2 tbsp cornstarch

CRUMBLE TOPPING
1 tbsp chopped pistachios
1 tbsp nibbed almonds
1 tbsp demerara sugar
1 tbsp rolled oats
1 tbsp desiccated coconut

10 free-range egg whites
⅓ cup superfine sugar, plus
   extra for dusting
unsalted butter, for greasing
clotted cream, for serving
   (optional)

*La découverte d'un mets nouveau
fait plus pour le bonheur du genre
humain que la découverte d'une étoile*

The discovery of a new dish confers
more happiness on humanity than
the discovery of a new star

JEAN ANTHELME BRILLAT-SAVARIN

Riz impératrice

EMPRESS RICE PUDDING

This old-fashioned rice dessert is timeless in my view
and is a long way away from the stodgy rice pudding
that's often passed off as a classic. There's quite a bit
of work involved, but it's well worth it.

First soak the dried fruit. Make a sugar syrup by boiling 1 cup water with
the ½ cup sugar, then add the fruit, pistachios, and a splosh of Kirsch
to taste. Leave for a couple of hours or overnight.

Put the rice in a pan and cover with plenty of water. Bring it to a boil and
cook for 5 minutes, then drain. Tip the rice back into the pan with the milk,
split vanilla pod, and ¼ cup sugar. Simmer until all the liquid has been
absorbed, then cover and let cool.

To make the crème anglaise, whisk the egg yolks and sugar in a bowl. Bring
the milk to a boil, pour it onto the eggs and sugar and mix well. Return the
mixture to the pan and cook gently until thickened. Do not let it boil, or the
eggs will scramble.

Put the gelatin in a dish of cold water to soften, then squeeze dry and add it
to the hot crème anglaise. Pass the mixture through a sieve – set the vanilla
pod aside to use as decoration if you like. When the crème is cool, add it to
the rice mix, then fold in the whipped cream.

Lightly oil a mold such as a 1.5-quart pudding steamer. Pour in half the rice
mixture, add some of the drained, soaked fruit (reserving the rest and the
syrup), then cover with the remaining mixture.

Leave the pudding in the fridge to set overnight, then decorate with a few
of the soaked fruits. Serve with the rest of the fruit and syrup.

SERVES 10—12

DRIED FRUIT
½ cup superfine sugar
6 oz mixed dried fruit
   (apricots, prunes,
   cherries, to taste)
2 tbsp pistachio nuts
Kirsch, to taste

⅔ cup Arborio rice
1½ cups milk
1 vanilla pod, split
¼ cup superfine sugar

CRÈME ANGLAISE
4 medium free-range
   egg yolks
½ cup superfine sugar
1½ cups milk
3 gelatin sheets
1 cup whipping cream,
   whipped
vegetable oil, for greasing

Millefeuille à la mangue et grenade

MILLEFEUILLE WITH MANGO AND POMEGRANATE

The seasoning of the mango is vital to this dessert.
In the tropics, mangoes and pineapples are often served
sprinkled with pepper or chile – both a perfect foil for
the fragrant flowery sweetness of these fruits. For this
recipe you need mangoes that are ripe enough to taste
good, but not so ripe that you can't slice them neatly.
If you can't manage the mango curls, don't worry – cut
your mangoes into matchsticks and the millefeuille will
still taste delicious.

Roll out the puff pastry on a lightly floured surface to form a rectangle
1/16 inch thick. Place the pastry on a baking sheet and leave in the fridge
to rest for 30 minutes.

Preheat the oven to 425°F. Prick the pastry at intervals with a fork to
prevent it from shrinking as it cooks. Place a sheet of parchment paper
on top, followed by another baking sheet to keep the pastry flat. Bake for
10 minutes, then remove the sheet and paper. Turn the oven temperature
down to 400°F and cook the pastry until crisp and cooked through, another
20 minutes. Remove from the oven and carefully slip the pastry onto a wire
rack to cool. Cut the pastry into 12 rectangles, each 3 x 1½ inches.

To make the crème pâtissière, whisk the eggs with the sugar in a bowl and
add the flour. Bring the milk to a boil and pour it into the bowl, mixing
well. Tip the mixture back into the saucepan and bring it to a boil, whisking
constantly. Remove from the heat as soon as it boils and dust the surface
with a little confectioners' sugar to avoid a crust or skin forming. Once the
crème is completely cold, fold in the whipped cream.

Skin the mangoes, slice them, and season with the lime zest, half the lime
juice, and the piment d'Espelette. Roll the slices into curls as neatly as you
can. To make the sauce, blitz all the mango trimmings with the superfine
sugar and the rest of the lime juice until smooth.

To assemble, take a pastry rectangle and pipe a little crème pâtissière over
it. Add some mango curls and pomegranate seeds and then repeat, finishing
with a layer of pastry. Dust with confectioners' sugar or add some spun sugar
or tiny brandy snaps if you like. Serve with the mango sauce.

SERVES 4

8 oz all-butter puff pastry
all-purpose flour, for rolling
6 ripe mangoes
 grated zest of 1 lime and
    juice of 2
1 tsp ground piment
    d'Espelette (chile powder)
¼ cup superfine sugar
seeds from 1 fresh
    pomegranate
confectioners' sugar,
    for dusting

CRÈME PÂTISSIÈRE

3 medium free-range
    egg yolks
¼ cup superfine sugar
¼ cup (1 oz) all-purpose
    flour
¾ cup milk
6 tbsp heavy cream,
    whipped

spun sugar (see page 278),
    for serving (optional)
brandy snaps or honey tuiles
    (see page 341), for serving
    (optional)

Fraises Sarah Bernhardt

STRAWBERRIES SARAH BERNHARDT

I couldn't write a book of French classics without doffing my chef's hat to this wonderful dessert, created by Escoffier for the famous actress of the day. You can serve this in one large bowl, but it looks wonderfully retro in individual glasses.

To make the pineapple sorbet, peel the pineapple and dice the flesh. Put this in a pan with the sugar, glucose, and lemon juice and bring it to a boil, then blitz until smooth in a food processor. Freeze in an ice-cream machine. Alternatively, you can spoon the mixture onto a tray, cover, and leave in the freezer to set, mixing every 30 minutes until smooth.

To make the mousse, whisk the yolks and sugar together in a bowl. Bring the milk to a boil with the orange peel, then pour this onto the yolks and mix well. Tip the mixture back into the pan and cook carefully until it thickens. Place the gelatin in a saucer of cold water until it softens, then squeeze out the excess water. Add the softened gelatin and the Curaçao to the egg mixture, then pass through a fine sieve. Let cool and, when almost set, fold in the whipped cream. Refrigerate until firm.

Hull the strawberries and cut them in halves or quarters if large. Douse with the brandy and Curaçao, then cover and refrigerate for at least an hour.

To serve, spoon some of the pineapple sorbet into each dish followed by the strawberries and juices, then top with some Curaçao mousse. Decorate with some spun sugar (below) if you like.

To make spun sugar, melt superfine sugar in a frying pan until it turns golden brown – watch it carefully and don't let it burn. Remove the pan from the heat and use a fork to flick the sugar back and forth over a greased wooden spoon or ladle to make a fragile cage.

SERVES 6

PINEAPPLE SORBET

1 sweet, golden pineapple
a third of the pineapple's peeled weight in superfine sugar
2 tbsp liquid glucose
1 lemon juice

CURAÇAO MOUSSE

3 medium free-range egg yolks
1/3 cup superfine sugar
1 cup milk
2 thinly pared strips of orange peel
2 gelatin sheets
4 tbsp Curaçao
6 tbsp whipping cream, whipped

1 lb strawberries
2 tbsp brandy
4 tbsp Curaçao

SPUN SUGAR (OPTIONAL)

1 cup superfine sugar

Galette serpentine

ALMOND PUFF PASTRY

This is a lost version of the famous *pithiviers* — a different shape, but just as delicious. It's best served warm from the oven, and is perfect for teatime.

To make the almond cream, beat the butter until it's smooth and creamy, then whisk in the ground almonds and confectioners' sugar. Beat in the eggs, one at a time, and once they are all incorporated, add the rum.

Roll out the puff pastry to a strip measuring about 5 inches wide and 20 inches long. Trim the edges so the strip is perfectly straight. Pipe the almond cream down the middle of the strip, then lightly brush one edge with beaten egg and fold over to seal. Make sure there are no air pockets.

Preheat the oven to 425°F. Make little cuts ¼ inch apart all the way along the sealed edge of the strip. Arrange the strip in a spiral on a nonstick baking sheet, with the cut edge facing out. Brush with beaten egg and cook for 10 minutes, then turn down the oven to 400°F until the galette is cooked through, another 20 minutes. Take the galette out of the oven and carefully slide it onto a wire rack to cool slightly before serving.

SERVES 10

ALMOND CREAM

⅔ cup soft unsalted butter
1⅓ cups ground almonds
1 cups plus 6 tbsp
    confectioners' sugar
3 medium free-range eggs
1 tbsp rum

14 oz all-butter puff pastry
2 free-range egg yolks,
    beaten, for brushing

Charlotte aux poires

PEAR CHARLOTTE

This is a boozy delight and takes me back to my days as an apprentice when charlottes were in fashion. All kinds of flavors and perfumes were used, but my all-time favorite is this pear version. I use canned pears, which may come as a surprise, but they work beautifully.

First make the biscuit for lining a charlotte mold or a loose-based 8-inch cake pan. Separate the eggs and whisk the yolks with ⅔ cup of the superfine sugar until pale. Whisk the whites until frothy, add the remaining superfine sugar and whisk again until firm. Gently fold this into the yolk mixture. Once nearly all the egg white is incorporated, fold in the flour – take care not to overmix.

Put the biscuit mixture in a piping bag. Pipe a circle of dots onto a nonstick baking mat. The circle should be the same diameter as the mold and the dots should be touching. Next pipe another circle in a spiral onto another mat to form the base of the charlotte. Pipe the rest of the mixture in diagonal strips onto a separate nonstick baking mat, piping the strips close together so they touch. Dust with confectioners' sugar and bake all the biscuit at 400°F until cooked, 12 minutes. Let cool.

Set the circles aside. Cut out sections of the diagonal strips the same depth as the mold to line the sides. Line the base of your mold with the biscuit spiral, then line the sides with sections of the diagonal strips, making sure there are no gaps. Moisten with a little of the pear syrup and eau-de-vie.

Now make a bavarois mixture. Place the gelatin in iced water to soften. Whisk the yolks and superfine sugar in a bowl until pale. Pour the pear syrup into a saucepan, then add the milk powder and vanilla pod and bring to a boil. Pour the boiling pear milk onto the yolks, mix well, then tip back into the pan and cook until it's thickened and coats the back of a spoon. Once the mixture reaches 179°F (check with a thermometer) remove from the heat and add the drained, squeezed gelatin. Pass through a fine sieve and let cool a little before adding the pear eau-de-vie. Cover with plastic wrap and chill.

Once the mixture is cold and semi-set, fold in the whipped cream. Pour half the mixture into the lined mold, add plenty of chopped pear, then pour on the rest of the bavarois. Let cool overnight, then top with the circle of biscuit dots and serve. This also freezes well, so can be made in advance.

SERVES 12

BISCUIT CUILLÈRE
9 medium free-range eggs
1⅓ cups superfine sugar
2⅓ cups (9½ oz)
    all-purpose flour
6 tbsp confectioners' sugar,
    for dusting

4 gelatin sheets (bronze)
6 medium free-range egg
    yolks
¼ cup superfine sugar
1 cup pear syrup from
    the can
¼ cup milk powder
1 vanilla pod, split
¾ cup poire Williams
    eau-de-vie
1½ cups whipping cream,
    whipped
8½ oz canned pears,
    chopped

Tarte au chocolat

WARM BITTER CHOCOLATE TART

Use the best chocolate you can get for making this tart, as it really is worth it. And yes, it does contain a lot of butter, but it is very special. It's great for a party as you can make it the day before and keep it in the fridge, but do warm it through gently and serve it tepid.

To make the pastry, cut the butter into small pieces and leave it to soften at room temperature. Sift the flour and salt, place them on the work surface, and make a well in the center. Add the butter and sugar and gently work together with your fingertips. Add the egg yolk and gradually draw in the flour, adding drops of water as you go. When all the flour has been incorporated, shape the dough into a ball, but do not overwork it. Wrap the pastry in plastic wrap and refrigerate for at least 2 hours before using.

To make the bitter orange sauce, boil the orange juice and sugar until reduced by three-quarters. Add the marmalade, stir until it has melted, then pass the sauce through a fine sieve. Let cool.

Preheat the oven to 350°F. Roll out the pastry and use it to line a 10½-inch flan pan. Cover the base of the pastry with parchment paper and add some dried beans, then bake for 20 minutes. Remove the beans and paper and return the pastry to the oven for 5 minutes to cook completely. Turn the oven down to 275°F.

Whisk the whole eggs, yolks, and sugar with an electric mixer at full speed until pale and frothy, about 5 minutes. Melt the chocolate and butter in a bowl set over a pan of simmering water, then fold into the egg mixture. Pour this onto the pastry base, place the tart in the oven immediately, and bake for 15 minutes. Remove and let cool to tepid before serving with the bitter orange sauce and, if you like, some ice cream.

SERVES 8

SWEET PASTRY

5 tbsp unsalted butter
1 cup (4½ oz) all-purpose
  flour, plus extra
  for dusting
pinch salt
2 tbsp sugar
1 free-range egg yolk
1 tbsp water

BITTER ORANGE SAUCE

¾ cup fresh orange juice
½ cup superfine sugar
2 tbsp bitter orange
  marmalade

3 free-range eggs
4 free-range egg yolks
¾ cup superfine sugar
13 oz bitter chocolate
  (70% cocoa solids),
  roughly chopped
1 cup unsalted butter, cubed
ice cream (see pages
  294–296), for serving
  (optional)

Poires pochées aux amandes et chocolat

POACHED PEARS WITH CHOCOLATE ALMOND SAUCE

Pears and chocolate are a fabulous combination and one of my favorites. Serve these pears warm with the chocolate sauce and, if feeling particularly indulgent, some whipped cream.

Put the sugar, scraped vanilla pod, and seeds with 2 cups water in a pan and bring to a boil. Peel the pears and remove their cores from the base, then place them in the simmering syrup. Cover with parchment paper and cook until a knife pierces the pear easily – the exact time will depend on the ripeness of the pear. Leave the pears in the syrup to cool slightly while you make the sauce.

To make the sauce, boil 1 cup water with the cocoa powder and sugar, while whisking vigorously. Take the pan off the heat and whisk in the butter and chocolate, then add the almonds. Serve with the poached pears.

SERVES 4

1½ cup superfine sugar
1 vanilla pod, split and
    seeds scraped out
4 pears (Williams or
    similar)
whipped cream (optional)

CHOCOLATE ALMOND SAUCE
¾ cup unsweetened cocoa
    powder
½ cup superfine sugar
2 tbsp unsalted butter
1–2 oz bitter chocolate,
    broken into pieces
⅓ cup almonds, toasted
    and chopped

On doit aimer soit ce qu'on va manger, soit la personne pour laquelle on cuisine. Ensuite, vous devez vous donner à la cuisine – la cuisine est un acte d'amour

You have to love either what you are going to eat, or the person you are cooking for. Then you have to give yourself up to the cooking – cooking is an act of love

ALAIN CHAPEL

Petits pots de crème

LITTLE CREAM POTS

Like crème brûlée and crème caramel, these little
desserts are set custards and are baked in individual
pots, traditionally with their own lids. If you do not
have pots with lids, you can cover the custards with foil,
making a little hole to allow steam to escape. I find that
little glass yogurt pots are ideal.

SERVES 8

3 free-range eggs
4 free-range egg yolks
½ cup superfine sugar
1 cup milk
1 cup light cream
1 vanilla pod, split and seeds
   scraped out
Chantilly cream (see
   page 340), for serving
   (optional)

Preheat the oven to 350°F. Whisk the eggs and yolks with the sugar until pale.
Bring the milk and cream to a boil with the vanilla pod and seeds, then pour
this onto the egg mixture and whisk well. Pass the custard through a sieve and
pour it into little pots or cups. Carefully remove all the froth from the tops
and put on the lids or foil. Make a little hole in the foil tops, if using.

Place the pots in an ovenproof dish and pour in enough hot water to reach
about a third of the way up the sides of the dish. Bake in the oven until set,
about 30 minutes depending on the size. Smaller pots won't take quite as
long. Traditionally these simple little sweets are served just as they are, but if
you want to dress them up, pipe a little rosette of Chantilly cream on top.

PETITS POTS DE CRÈME AU CHOCOLAT

For a chocolate version, stir 6 oz bitter chocolate (70% cocoa solids) into the
boiling milk and cream.

If you would like to make some of each type, divide the mixture in half and
add just 3 oz chocolate to one half.

Iles flottantes et compote de fraises

FLOATING ISLANDS WITH STRAWBERRY COMPOTE

Floating islands, without the strawberries, is a traditional Easter dessert in France and one my mother always used to make. But it is so good I love to eat it at any time of year, and with strawberry compote it has become a summertime favorite of Le Gavroche clients.

To make the strawberry compote, tip the washed and hulled strawberries into a pan and sprinkle them with a little sugar. The exact amount of sugar depends on the sweetness of the berries. Bring this to a boil, then immediately take off the heat, cover, and let cool.

To make the crème anglaise, bring the milk to a boil with the vanilla pod. Remove the pan from the heat, cover, and let infuse for 10 minutes. Beat the egg yolks with the ½ cup sugar until thick and creamy. Bring the milk back to a boil and pour it onto the yolk mixture, whisking continuously. Pour the mixture back into the saucepan and cook over low heat, stirring continuously with a spatula, until the custard thickens slightly.

To make the meringue, beat the egg whites with a whisk until frothy, then add the 1½ cups superfine sugar. Continue to whisk until the meringue is firm and smooth.

Bring a large pan of water, sweetened with 2 tablespoons of the remaining superfine sugar, to simmering point. Using a big kitchen spoon dipped in cold water, scoop out a big island of meringue and plunge the spoon into the simmering water. The island should come off the spoon into the water and poach in this liquid. Flip it over after 3–4 minutes to cook on the other side. Continue until all the egg whites are used.

Once cooked, gently take the islands out of the liquid with a slotted spoon and place them on a rack to cool and drain. When they're cold, heat the rest of the superfine sugar in a heavy pan until liquid and golden, then pour this caramel over the top of each island.

To serve, place some compote in each bowl, followed by crème anglaise, and finally the caramel-coated floating islands.

SERVES 4

STRAWBERRY COMPOTE
1 lb strawberries, washed and hulled
½ cup sugar, or to taste

CRÈME ANGLAISE
2 cups milk
1 vanilla pod, split
6 free-range egg yolks
½ cup superfine sugar

MERINGUE
6 free-range egg whites
1½ cups superfine sugar

1½ cups superfine sugar

Gâteau de riz au bain marie

BATH PUDDING

This is a recipe that dates back to the mid 1700s and it was probably named "Bath Pudding" because it was cooked in a bath of water, rather than after the town. Lovely served with some warm fruit compote.

SERVES 6–8

1/3 cup Arborio rice

2 scant cups milk

1 pinch salt

1/4 cup heavy cream

thinly pared peel of
    1/2 lemon

unsalted butter, for greasing

2 free-range eggs

1 free-range egg yolk

1/3 cup sugar

finely grated zest of
    1/2 lemon

raspberry jam, melted

Grind the rice in a food processor until it is the texture of fine semolina. Mix a little of the milk with the ground rice and a pinch of salt to make a paste.

Bring the rest of the milk and cream to a boil, with the thinly pared lemon peel. Pour this onto the rice paste and stir well, then tip it all back into the pan and bring to a boil. Let cool for about 10 minutes, then remove the peel.

Butter a 3-cup jelly mold or pudding steamer. Whisk the whole eggs, yolk, sugar, and grated lemon zest in a large bowl, then stir in the rice mixture and mix well. Pour the mixture into the buttered mold or basin and cover with foil. Place the bowl in a saucepan and add hot water to come about halfway up the sides. Bring the water to a boil, then simmer gently until the pudding is set, 1 1/2 hours. Let cool for a few moments before turning out.

Brush with some melted jam and serve.

Clafoutis aux pruneaux

PRUNE CLAFOUTIS

A family favorite and a dish that my grandma used to cook. Cherry clafoutis is the classic version, but when cherries are not in season, make this clafoutis with prunes instead. It's equally delicious, and even better if you soak the prunes in a good splosh of brandy the day before making the clafoutis.

Lightly butter a 9-inch flan dish and preheat the oven to 350°F. Put the prunes in the dish.

Whisk the eggs and sugar in a bowl until light and pale in color. Add the scrapings of the vanilla pod and the sifted flour, then slowly pour in the milk without overwhisking and add the melted butter. Pass the mixture through a fine sieve, then pour it into the dish over the prunes. Cook the clafoutis until puffed up and set, 30 minutes.

SERVES 6–8

2 tbsp unsalted butter, melted, plus extra for greasing
30 prunes, pitted
3 free-range eggs
1/3 cup superfine sugar
1 vanilla pod, split and seeds scraped out
1/4 cup (1 oz) all-purpose flour, sifted
1 1/2 cups milk

Glace à la vanille

VANILLA ICE CREAM

Bring the milk to a boil with the vanilla pods, then remove the pan from the heat, cover, and let infuse for 10 minutes.

Beat the egg yolks with the sugar until thick and creamy. Bring the milk back to a boil and pour it onto the yolk mixture, whisking continuously. Pour the mixture back into the saucepan and cook over low heat, stirring constantly with a spatula until the custard thickens slightly. Stir in the vanilla extract and pass through a fine sieve. Chill, then churn in an ice-cream machine until frozen.

SERVES 12

1 quart whole milk

4 vanilla pods, split

12 free-range egg yolks

1 cup superfine sugar

2 tsp vanilla extract

Glace aux pruneaux et Armagnac

PRUNE AND ARMAGNAC ICE CREAM

Prepare the prunes a week ahead. Remove the pits and put the prunes in a bowl, then sprinkle them with sugar and douse with the Armagnac. Cover tightly and refrigerate.

When you're ready to make the ice cream, drain the prunes and add the liquid to the ice cream mixture and churn as above. Just before serving, remove the ice cream from the freezer and leave until it becomes pliable, then fold in the roughly chopped prunes.

SERVES 12

6 Agen prunes

2 tbsp demerara sugar

½ cup Armagnac

1 recipe vanilla ice cream
  mixture (see above)

Glace au beurre noisette

BROWN BUTTER ICE CREAM

Heat the sugar in a pan until brown and caramelized. Add ⅔ cup water, the milk, and the cream, and bring to a boil – take care when adding the liquid to the hot sugar, as it may bubble up fiercely.

Heat the butter in a separate pan until it starts to brown. Leave it to cool slightly, then add the cornstarch, egg yolks, and liquid glucose and whisk well. Pour in the caramel mixture, whisking constantly, then cook over low heat until the custard thickens slightly. Keep stirring with a spatula. Pass the mixture through a fine sieve, then chill and churn it in an ice-cream machine until frozen.

For salted caramel ice cream, use good salted butter or add 2 teaspoons of flaked sea salt to the custard mixture.

SERVES 12

1 cup plus 3 tbsp superfine sugar
2½ cups milk
2½ cups heavy cream
1 cup plus 3 tbsp unsalted butter
2 tbsp cornstarch
9 free-range egg yolks
¼ cup liquid glucose

Glaces aux bananes et rhum

BANANA AND RUM ICE CREAM

If the bananas are not fully ripe, leave them in a warm place or even put them in a very low oven for 3 hours.

Peel the bananas and blitz them in a food processor or blender with the sugar, rum, and lemon juice. Slowly add the cream, blending until smooth. Pour the mixture into an ice-cream machine and churn until frozen.

SERVES 12

2 lb very ripe bananas (peeled weight)
3 cups superfine sugar
¾ cup good-quality dark rum
juice of 1 lemon
1 quart light cream

Glace aux pistaches

PISTACHIO ICE CREAM

Put the egg yolks and half the sugar into a large bowl and whisk until thick and creamy. Bring the milk and the remaining sugar to a boil, then remove from the heat, add the pistachio paste, and stir to dissolve. Pour the hot milk into the yolk mixture and stir well. Pour the mixture back into the saucepan and stir over low heat until the mixture thickens enough to coat the spoon.

Let cool, then strain the mixture into an ice-cream machine and churn until frozen but not too stiff. Stir in the pistachios and freeze until needed.

SERVES 8

6 free-range egg yolks
½ cup superfine sugar
2 cups whole milk
2 tbsp pistachio paste
3 tbsp peeled pistachios, roughly chopped

Glace au miel

HONEY ICE CREAM

Bring the milk to a boil in a saucepan. Meanwhile, whisk the eggs with the honey until thick and creamy, then slowly whisk in the cream. Pour the boiling milk onto the yolk mixture and whisk vigorously. Strain the mixture through a sieve and let cool. Chill, then churn in an ice-cream machine until frozen.

SERVES 8

2 cups milk
4 free-range egg yolks
1 cup flower-scented clear honey
1¼ cups heavy cream

Sorbet au chocolat amer

BITTER CHOCOLATE SORBET

Bring 3 cups water to a boil with the sugar, glucose, and cocoa powder, whisking well to dissolve. Add the chopped chocolate and bring to a boil again. Let cool and then churn in an ice-cream machine until frozen.

SERVES 12

1 cup superfine sugar

1/3 cup liquid glucose

1²/₃ cups cocoa powder

5 oz extra bitter chocolate (70% cocoa solids), chopped

Le trou Gascon

ARMAGNAC SORBET

This sorbet can be served in the middle of a meal to refresh and cleanse the palate, or as a dessert with some fresh grapes that have been peeled and steeped in Armagnac.

Pour 2 cups water into a pan, add the sugar, and glucose, and bring to a boil, stirring occasionally to dissolve the sugar. Boil for 3 minutes. Add 1 cup water and the wine and Armagnac to the boiling syrup, then remove from the heat, cover, and let cool. When cold, churn in an ice-cream machine until frozen, then serve immediately.

SERVES 8

2¹/₂ cups sugar

1/4 cup liquid glucose

1 cup dry white wine

1 cup Armagnac

In France, bread is thought of as more than food;
it is a symbol of life itself, and must be given proper
respect. Bread should never be placed upside down
on the table, for example – that could bring bad luck.
A French meal is not complete without bread and it's
served at every opportunity, to savor, enjoy – and to
mop up the juices on the plate. The French will even
eat bread with bread! Bakers bake throughout the
day and many people will visit their local bakery at
least a couple of times a day to buy the freshest loaves,
warm from the oven.

Pain et croissants

Fougasse

OLIVE FLATBREAD

A Mediterranean-style flatbread, *fougasse* is excellent
served with tapenade or vegetable soups.

Dissolve the yeast in a little of the warm water in a large bowl. Add the flour,
salt, the rest of the water, and the olive oil, then knead until the dough is
smooth and very elastic – this will take about 10 minutes. Cover the dough
with a damp cloth and leave it to rise in a warm place until doubled in size,
about an hour.

Knead the dough again briefly and add the olives. Roll it out on a floured
surface to form a rough leaf shape, about ¾ inch thick, and place this on
a baking sheet. Using a sharp knife, cut 6 or 7 slits in the dough and open
them up so you can see the baking sheet.

Preheat the oven to 475°F. Brush the dough lightly with the beaten egg,
sprinkle with coarse salt, and bake until golden brown, about 9 minutes.
Let cool on a wire rack.

MAKES 1 LARGE LOAF

¾ oz (20 g) fresh yeast
1½ cups warm water
   (110–115°F)
4 cups (17 oz) multi-grain
   flour, plus extra for rolling
1 tsp salt
4 tbsp olive oil
⅓ cup good-quality olives,
   pitted and cut in half
1 free-range egg, beaten
coarse sea salt

Pissaladière

ONION AND OLIVE TART

This variation on pizza is popular in southern France and has a puff pastry base instead of dough. It's simple to make, but do allow plenty of time for the onions to cook so they are really tender and sticky.

Cut the onions in half and slice them very thinly. Heat 2 tablespoons olive oil in a large, heavy-bottomed pan over medium heat and add the onions, bay leaf, and thyme. Season lightly with salt, generously with pepper, then cook stirring frequently, until the onions are very tender, sweet and light brown in color, 35–40 minutes. Let cool.

Roll out the pastry into a circle that's $1/16$–$1/8$ inch thick and fold over the edges to make a raised rim. Prick the base with a fork and lightly brush the edges with the beaten egg. Refrigerate for an hour.

Preheat the oven to 475°F. Spread the onions thickly over the pastry base and arrange the olives and anchovies on top. Cook until the pastry is a light golden color, about 15 minutes. Brush the pissaladière with olive oil and serve warm.

SERVES 4

6 large onions, peeled
olive oil
1 bay leaf
3–4 sprigs of thyme
7 oz puff pastry
1 free-range egg, beaten
30 black olives (preferably Niçoise)
12 salted anchovy fillets
salt
black pepper

Pain aux ceps et l'ail confit

PORCINI AND GARLIC BREAD

This wonderful bread is flavored with dried porcini and the delicate sweetness of confit garlic – garlic cloves cooked slowly and gently in olive oil. Good served on its own or with a seasonal salad.

Cover the porcini with ⅔ cup of the warm water and leave them to soak for 30 minutes. Dissolve the yeast in the rest of the warm water in a large bowl, then stir in the white bread flour with a wooden spatula. Cover and leave in a warm place to rise and double in volume. Drain the porcini (reserving the liquid) and fry them in the olive oil for 1 minute. Drain again and set aside.

In the bowl of a stand mixer, put the soaking water of the porcini, the spelt and rye flours, thyme leaves, a pinch of salt, and the risen first dough. Knead at a low speed with the dough hook for 10 minutes. Scrape down the dough from the edges of the bowl and knead for another 2 minutes. Cover and let rise for 30 minutes.

Punch down the dough, then gently work in the porcini and confit garlic cloves (below) without breaking them up. Do this by folding the bread over on itself several times. Shape the dough into a loaf and place it on a floured baking sheet, then cover and let rise for 30 minutes. Preheat the oven to 425°F and bake the loaf for 35–40 minutes. Let cool on a wire rack.

CONFIT GARLIC

Separate the garlic cloves, peel them, and blanch in boiling water. Drain and put the cloves on a piece of foil, sprinkle with sea salt and a generous amount of olive oil, then wrap up in the foil to make a loose "bag." Place this on a baking sheet and bake in the oven at 350°F for about 30 minutes. Shake the garlic in the foil "bag" a few times during the cooking. Let cool before using.

MAKES 1 LARGE LOAF

⅔ cup dried porcini
1¾ cups warm water
   (110–115°F)
¾ oz (25 g) fresh yeast
3⅓ cups (14 oz) white
   bread flour, plus
   extra for dusting
1 tbsp olive oil
1 cup (3½ oz) spelt flour
1 cup (3½ oz) rye flour
1 tbsp thyme leaves, picked
   from the stems
12 confit garlic cloves
   (see below)
salt

CONFIT GARLIC

1 garlic bulb
olive oil
sea salt

Pain à l'huile d'olive

OLIVE OIL BREAD

This simple white bread is similar to a baguette, and is great for sandwiches. It also makes good croutons, as it crisps up well in the oven.

Dissolve the yeast in the warm water, add the flour, and knead until silky and elastic, 15 minutes. Add the olive oil and fine salt, then knead again for 5 minutes. Cover the dough and leave it to rise for 40 minutes.

Punch down the dough and form it into a long loaf. Place this on a nonstick baking sheet, cover, and let rise for another 20 minutes. Preheat the oven to 425°F. Lightly brush the top of the loaf with milk and add a sprinkling of coarse sea salt, then place it in the oven and bake until cooked through, 30 minutes. Let cool on a wire rack.

MAKES 1 LOAF

½ oz (12 g) fresh yeast

1 cup warm water (110–115°F)

4 cups (17 oz) unbleached stone-ground bread flour

4 tbsp olive oil

1 heaping tsp fine salt

milk, for brushing

1 pinch coarse sea salt

Brioche

RICH SWEET BREAD

Brioche dough is enriched with eggs so is richer than croissants. It makes a delicious cake-like bread that is good served at breakfast – or any other time of day. It's excellent with savory terrines too.

Place the yeast in a stand mixer bowl with a few drops of warm water to soften it. Add the sifted flour, 6 of the eggs (one at a time), and the salt and sugar, then slowly knead with the dough attachment. You can do this by hand, but you get a better result with a machine.

After 5 minutes, the dough should be smooth and elastic. Add the softened butter and continue to knead at a slightly faster speed for 10 minutes. Make sure all the butter has been incorporated. Put the dough in a large, clean container, cover it with plastic wrap, and leave it in the fridge for 12 hours. After 4 hours, punch the dough firmly to release the fermentation gases.

Tip the brioche dough out onto a floured surface and roll it into a loaf pan or shape it into 30 balls and place them on a baking sheet. Leave in a warm, draft-free place until risen by a third. Preheat the oven to 400°F. Beat the remaining egg and use it to brush the surface of the brioche, then cook until golden. A loaf will take about 40 minutes to cook, and small brioche rolls about 15 minutes.

MAKES 1 LARGE LOAF
OR 30 SMALL BUNS

½ oz (15 g) fresh yeast

4 cups (17 oz) all-purpose flour, sifted, plus extra for dusting

7 free-range eggs

2 tsp salt

¼ cup sugar

1 cup plus 3 tbsp softened unsalted butter

Croissants

CROISSANTS

Every bakery in France displays trays of freshly baked croissants for that quick morning mouthful with a cup of coffee. If you've never made your own it's well worth a try, and once you get the knack of folding them correctly it's not that hard. You can also freeze the croissants once rolled, and then whip them out of the freezer an hour before cooking. Enjoy them warm from the oven.

Dissolve the yeast in the warm water and milk powder. Add this to the sifted flour, sugar, salt, and the 3 tablespoons melted butter. Knead well by hand or machine for 4–5 minutes until the dough is smooth and everything is incorporated, but do not overwork. Cover and leave the dough to rise until doubled in size.

Roll the dough out to about legal paper size. Place the room-temperature butter in the middle and fold over the edges of the dough to enclose the butter completely. Dust the dough with flour and gently roll it out to a rectangle measuring about 15 x 10 inches. Take both ends, fold them to the center and fold again to make a much smaller rectangle. Wrap in plastic wrap and refrigerate for an hour, then repeat the process of rolling out and folding the dough.

Roll the dough out on a floured surface to a thickness of ⅜ inch and cut it into 30 triangles, each with a base of 5 inches. Roll each triangle towards the point, then bring the points together to form the croissant shape. Place the croissants on a baking sheet and leave them to rise for about 20 minutes. Preheat the oven to 350°F.

Brush the croissants with beaten egg and bake for 15 minutes until cooked.

MAKES 30 SMALL CROISSANTS

1½ oz (45 g) fresh yeast
1⅔ cups warm water (110–115°F)
6 tbsp milk powder
6½ cups (28 oz) all-purpose flour, sifted, plus extra for dusting
6 tbsp sugar
4 tsp salt
3 tbsp unsalted butter, melted
1 cup plus 3 tbsp unsalted butter, at room temperature
1 free-range egg, beaten

Pain de mie au lait

SANDWICH BREAD LOAF

Easy to make, this bread tastes great and is very satisfying. You can vary the recipe as you like and add wheatgerm, bran and a little rye or whole-grain flour instead of some of the white. A few cumin seeds mixed through the dough are also a good addition. If you are lactose intolerant, use water instead of the milk and oil instead of butter, but this does make it less rich. You will need 2 loaf tins measuring about 8 by 5 inches.

Dissolve the yeast in the warm milk in a large bowl, then add all the other ingredients. Mix thoroughly until lump free, then cover the dough and leave for 5 minutes.

Turn the dough out on a lightly floured surface and knead it for 10 minutes until smooth and elastic. Put the dough back in the bowl, cover and let ferment and rise for at least an hour or until almost doubled in size. Knock it back and shape it into 2 equal balls. Place these in lightly greased and floured bread tins, cover and let rise again.

Preheat the oven to 425°F. Using a razor blade or a very sharp knife, carefully slash the top of each loaf and immediately put them in the oven. After 10 minutes, turn down the oven to 350°F and continue to bake for 30 minutes. When cooked, tip the loaves out of the tins and leave them to cool on a wire rack.

MAKES 2 LOAVES

1 tbsp plus ½ tsp yeast

1½ cups warm milk

2 cups (8½ oz) all-purpose flour, plus extra for dusting

2 cups (8½ oz) bread flour

1 tbsp corn syrup

2 tsp sea salt

2 tbsp melted unsalted butter

En France, la cuisine est une sérieuse forme d'art et un sport national

In France, cooking is a serious
art form and a national sport

JULIA CHILD

Pain au cacao

CHOCOLATE BREAD

This sweet, bitter bread is perfect served with rich
winter dishes such as braised meats or game.

1 LOAF

5 tsp yeast

1½ cups warm water
  (110–115°F)

3⅓ cups (14 oz) white bread
  flour

1 cup extra-bitter cocoa
  powder, plus extra
  for dusting

1 tbsp brown sugar

1 tsp salt

Dissolve the yeast in a little of the warm water in a large bowl. Add the rest
of the ingredients and mix until the dough comes together, adding a couple
drops more water if needed. Knead for 10 minutes until the dough is supple
and elastic, then cover and let rise for an hour.

Knock the dough back and shape it into a round loaf. Cover and let rise again
until it has doubled in size, about 45 minutes. Preheat the oven to 475°F.
Dust the loaf with cocoa powder and carefully slash the top with a razor
blade or a very sharp knife. Cook for 20 minutes, then turn the oven down
to 350°F and cook for a further 30 minutes. Remove the bread and cool
on a wire rack.

Pain aux noix et yaourt

WALNUT AND YOGURT BREAD

This bread is quick and easy to make and is good with cheese or simply lashings of salted butter.

Mix all the dry ingredients together in a bowl. Put all the wet ingredients in a separate bowl and whisk, then combine the wet with the dry and mix well for 3–4 minutes. The dough should be fairly wet. Preheat the oven to 425°F.

Put the dough into a 2 nonstick loaf pan. Place it in the oven and immediately turn the heat down to 400°F and bake the loaf for an hour or until golden and fully cooked. Take the loaf out of the pan and let cool on a wire rack.

1 LOAF

3 cups (12½ oz) all-purpose flour

1 cup plus 2 tbsp whole-grain flour

1 tbsp bicarbonate of soda

1 tbsp baking powder

¾ cup chopped walnuts

½ tbsp honey

7 oz plain yogurt

1 tbsp vegetable oil

Pizza aux artichauts

ARTICHOKE PIZZA

This is not a classic Italian recipe, but one that I used to make when working as an apprentice in a pastry shop. The base is more like a rich brioche than pizza dough.

To make the dough, put the yeast in a bowl and pour on the water and milk. Mix well, then add the flour, salt, sugar, egg, and melted butter. Knead until the dough is elastic, shiny, and smooth, 4–5 minutes, then cover the bowl and refrigerate for at least 3 hours.

Next prepare the topping. Trim the artichokes and rub them with a cut lemon to prevent them from going brown. Thinly slice the onions and garlic. Heat a little olive oil in a pan and sear the sliced artichokes for 2–3 minutes, then add the onions and garlic. Once they have taken on a little color, season with salt and pepper and take the pan off the heat.

Take the dough out of the fridge and divide it into 8 balls. Place these on a floured surface, roll them out to about ¼ inch thick, and put them on a nonstick baking sheet. Divide the topping evenly over the bases, then leave for 20 minutes to rise. Preheat the oven to 475°F. Just before placing the pizzas in the oven, grate the cheese on top and drizzle with a little olive oil. Bake for about 10 minutes, then remove and serve.

SERVES 8

DOUGH

5 tsp yeast

¾ cup warm water (110–115°F)

¼ cup milk

4 cups (17 oz) bread flour, plus extra for dusting

2 tsp salt

1 tsp sugar

1 free-range egg, beaten

5 tbsp melted unsalted butter

TOPPING

8–12 small poivrade (purple) artichokes

1 lemon

2 large onions, peeled

3 garlic cloves, peeled

olive oil

2 very dry hard goat cheeses (crottin or Pélardon)

salt

black pepper

Pain Tunisien

SESAME-FLAVORED BREAD

This bread is perfect with all North African dishes, but give me some warm from the oven with just a few olives or dates or a hunk of good cheese and I'm happy.

Dissolve the yeast in the water, then add the semolina, flour, salt, and oil. Mix to form a dough, then knead until smooth and elastic, 10 minutes. Cover and let rise in a warm place until it has doubled in size, about an hour.

Punch down the dough, place it on a floured surface, and shape it into 2 balls. Using a rolling pin, roll these out into rounds about 8 inches across and 1¼ inches thick. Place them on a baking sheet, cover, and let double in size again. Preheat the oven to 425°F. Gently brush the dough with beaten egg and sprinkle with sesame seeds, then bake for 30 minutes.

2 SMALL LOAVES

5 tsp yeast

⅔ cup warm water (110–115°F)

1½ cups fine semolina (finest possible)

2 cups (8¾ oz) white bread flour, plus extra for dusting

1 tbsp salt

6 tbsp olive oil

1 free-range egg, beaten

2 tbsp sesame seeds

Stocks are the cornerstones of great cooking. You can buy good fresh stocks now, of course, but there's nothing like making your own for the best results. They're easy to prepare and allow you to make use of all the bones and trimmings from your meat and fish so there's no waste! I'm a big fan of sauces too, which can provide the finishing touch to a dish. Every keen cook should try to learn the basics, like a good meat jus and a classic hollandaise. You'll also find some other little extras in this chapter, which can help to make your cooking something special.

Bouillons et sauces

Bouillon de légumes

VEGETABLE STOCK

Peel or trim and roughly chop all the vegetables and put them in a large saucepan with 2½ quarts cold water. Add the herbs and bring the water to a boil. Simmer for about 35 minutes, then strain the stock before using. It can be kept in the fridge for up to 5 days, or it can be frozen.

MAKES 2 QUARTS

1 carrot

2 shallots

1 small onion

2 celery ribs

1 leek (green top part only)

1 bay leaf

1 bunch of thyme

a handful of parsley stalks

Bouillon de volaille

CHICKEN STOCK

Peel or trim and roughly chop all the vegetables and put them in a large saucepan. Add the bones or wing tips and the calf's foot, cover with 5 quarts water, and bring to a boil. Skim off the scum and fat that comes to the surface. Turn the heat down, add the herbs, and simmer for 1½ hours, skimming occasionally.

Pass the stock through a fine sieve and let cool. It can be kept in the fridge for up to 5 days, or it can be frozen.

MAKES ABOUT 4 QUARTS

1 onion

1 small leek

2 celery ribs

4 lb chicken bones or wing tips

1 calf's foot, split

2 sprigs of thyme

6 parsley stalks

Bouillon de volaille brun

BROWN CHICKEN STOCK

A brown chicken stock is used for soups, sauces, and other dishes that require a little extra depth and color, such as a consommé or a stew.

Preheat the oven to 425°F. Put the bones or wing tips and the calf's foot in a roasting pan, drizzle them with olive oil, and roast until brown. Transfer the bones to a deep saucepan, cover with 5 quarts of the cold water, and bring to a gentle simmer.

Meanwhile, place the roasting pan on the stove top, add the vegetables and garlic, then fry until golden. Add the tomato paste, thyme, and the remaining quart of water, then bring to a boil, stirring well to scrape up any caramelized bits sticking to the bottom of the pan. Once boiling, pour all the contents into the saucepan with the bones and continue to simmer for 2 hours, skimming when necessary. Pass the stock through a fine sieve and chill. The stock can be kept in the fridge for 5 days, or it can be frozen.

MAKES ABOUT 5 QUARTS

4 lb chicken bones or wing tips

1 calf's foot, split

olive oil

6 quarts cold water

1 onion, peeled and roughly chopped

1 carrot, peeled and roughly chopped

1 celery rib, roughly chopped

5 garlic cloves, peeled and roughly chopped

1 tbsp tomato paste

2 sprigs of thyme

Bouillon de canard

DUCK STOCK

Preheat the oven to 425°F. Put the bones and calf's foot in a roasting pan with a little oil and roast until well browned. Transfer them to a deep saucepan and cover with about 2 cups water.

Put the onion, carrot, and celery in the roasting pan and brown on the stove top, then add to the saucepan with the bones. Place the roasting pan over high heat and add 4 quarts cold water. Bring to a boil, scraping the bottom of the pan with a wooden spatula to loosen any caramelized bits, then pour the liquid into the saucepan with the bones.

Simmer for 2 hours, occasionally skimming off the fat and scum from the surface, then pass the stock through a sieve and chill. The stock can be kept in the fridge for up to 7 days, or it can be frozen.

MAKES ABOUT 3 QUARTS

4 lb duck bones
½ calf's foot, split
olive oil
1 onion, peeled and
    roughly chopped
1 carrot, peeled and
    roughly chopped
2 celery ribs, roughly
    chopped

Bouillon de veau

VEAL STOCK

Preheat the oven to 425°F. Put the bones and calf's foot in a roasting pan with a little oil and roast them in the oven, turning occasionally, until brown all over. Transfer them to a large saucepan.

Put the onion, carrots, and celery into the roasting pan and roast them in the oven until golden, turning frequently with a wooden spatula. Pour off any excess fat and put the vegetables into the saucepan with the bones. Place the roasting pan over high heat and add 2 cups water. Bring to a boil, scraping the bottom of the pan to loosen any caramelized bits, then pour everything into the saucepan with the bones.

Add the remaining ingredients and 4½ cups water and bring to a boil. Skim off the scum and fat, then turn down the heat and simmer gently for 3½ hours, skimming occasionally. Pass the stock through a fine sieve and let cool. The stock can be kept in the fridge for up to 7 days, or it can be frozen.

MAKES ABOUT 3½ QUARTS

3 lb veal knuckle bones,
    chopped
1 calf's foot, split
olive oil
1 large onion, peeled and
    roughly chopped
2 large carrots, peeled and
    roughly chopped
1 celery rib, roughly
    chopped
5 quarts water
2 garlic cloves, peeled
2 sprigs of thyme
½ tbsp tomato purée

Bouillon de boeuf

BEEF STOCK

Preheat the oven to 425°F. Put the bones and pigs' feet in a roasting pan with a little oil and roast them in the oven, turning occasionally, until brown all over. Transfer them to a large saucepan and pour in enough water to cover by 6 inches.

Pour off some of the fat from the roasting pan, add the onions, carrot, and celery, then roast until golden. Add the vegetables and all the other ingredients to the bones. Put the roasting pan over high heat. Pour in 2 cups water to deglaze the pan, scraping the bottom to loosen the caramelized bits, then pour into the pan with the bones. Bring to a boil, skim off the scum, then lower the heat and simmer for $2\frac{1}{2}$ hours, skimming frequently. Strain and chill. The stock can be kept in the fridge for up to 7 days, or it can be frozen.

MAKES ABOUT 5 QUARTS

6 lb beef bones, chopped

3 pigs' feet, split

olive oil

2 onions, peeled and
   roughly chopped

1 carrot, peeled and roughly
   chopped

2 celery ribs, roughly
   chopped

2 bay leaves

1 sprig of thyme

1 bunch of parsley stalks

2 tsp peppercorns

3 beefsteak tomatoes,
   chopped

1 leek top (green top
   part only)

Court bouillon

CLEAR POACHING STOCK

This is a perfect stock for poaching fish and for cooking lobsters. It can then be used as the basis of a fish stock or sauce.

Slice the vegetables into thin ⅛-inch rounds. Bring the water, wine, and vinegar to a boil, add all the vegetables, the bouquet garni, salt, and the peppercorns tied in a little muslin bag. Simmer until the vegetables are cooked but still a little crunchy, about 15 minutes. Strain and chill. This can be kept in the fridge for 3–4 days, or it can be frozen.

MAKES ABOUT 3½ QUARTS

2 carrots, peeled
white part of 1 leek
1 celery rib
½ fennel bulb
4 shallots, peeled
2 small white onions, peeled
1½ quarts water
1 bottle of dry white wine
2 tbsp white wine vinegar
1 bouquet garni
1½ tbsp coarse sea salt
1 tbsp cracked black or
   white peppercorns

Bouillon de poisson

FISH STOCK

Remove any gills from the fish heads, then soak the heads and bones in cold water for 3–4 hours. Remove them from the water and chop roughly. Melt the butter in a deep saucepan and sweat the onion and celery over low heat until softened. Add the fish bones and heads and cook for 2–3 minutes, stirring frequently.

Pour in the wine, turn up the heat and reduce by half. Add the water and herbs and bring to a boil, skimming frequently. Lower the heat and simmer, uncovered, for 25 minutes. Strain through a muslin-lined sieve and let cool. This can be kept in the fridge for 2–3 days, or it can be frozen.

MAKES ABOUT 2 QUARTS

2 lb bones and heads from
   white fish (sole, whiting,
   turbot)
4 tbsp unsalted butter
1 small onion, peeled and
   roughly chopped
1 celery rib, roughly
   chopped
¼ cup dry white wine
2 quarts water
6 parsley stalks
1 bay leaf

Bouillon de homard

LOBSTER STOCK

I've specified lobster heads because the claws and body have little flavor, although you can add them if you have room in the pan. Add langoustine and prawn heads too if you have them.

Crush the lobster heads with a mallet or a rolling pin until they are well broken up. Heat the olive oil in a large saucepan over medium heat and sweat the onion, carrot, and celery. When the vegetables are lightly browned, add the herbs and lobster heads, stirring to prevent them from sticking to the pan. After about 5 minutes, stir in the tomatoes, tomato purée, and cayenne pepper. Pour in the brandy and stir well for a couple of minutes, then add the wine and boil for at least 3 minutes.

Add the stocks and bring to a boil, then season lightly with sea salt. Simmer for 40 minutes, stirring occasionally and skimming off any scum that appears on the surface.

Drain the stock through a colander set over a large bowl, pressing the lobster heads well to extract all the juices and flavor. Then pass this liquid through a fine sieve into a clean saucepan, bring it to a boil and skim. The stock can be kept in the fridge for 2–3 days, or it can be frozen.

MAKES ABOUT 3 QUARTS

6 lb lobster heads

2 tbsp olive oil

1 large onion, peeled and chopped

1 carrot, peeled and chopped

2 celery ribs, chopped

4 parsley stalks

1 sprig of thyme

1 bay leaf

2 large tomatoes

2 tbsp tomato purée

$\frac{1}{2}$ tsp cayenne pepper

1 tbsp brandy

$1\frac{1}{4}$ cups dry white wine

2 quarts fish stock

1 quart veal stock (see page 322)

sea salt

Dans la cuisine, les sauces sont comme les premiers rudiments de grammaire – le fondement de toutes les langues

Sauces in cookery are like the first rudiments of grammar – the foundation of all languages

ALEXIS SOYER

Jus de volaille

CHICKEN JUS

While a stock is the foundation of a sauce, a jus has a more intense flavor and more body. It needs only a little butter or other finishing touch to make it into a sauce.

Preheat the oven to 425°F. Put the bones in a roasting pan and roast them in the oven, turning occasionally, until brown all over. Transfer the bones to a deep pan.

Brown the shallots in the roasting pan, stirring frequently. Add the wine and stir to loosen all the residue. Boil to reduce by half, then pour into the pan with the bones. Add the stock and bring to a boil. Simmer for 45 minutes, skimming occasionally, then strain.

MAKES ABOUT 2 QUARTS

2 lb chicken bones, chopped
  small
3 shallots, chopped
6 tbsp dry white wine
2½ quarts chicken stock
  (see page 320)

Jus de boeuf

BEEF JUS

Preheat the oven to 425°F. Put the bones or trimmings in a roasting pan and roast them in the oven, turning occasionally, until brown all over. Transfer them to a deep saucepan.

Brown the onion in the roasting pan, stirring frequently. Add the wine and stir to loosen all the caramelized bits on the bottom of the pan. Boil to reduce by half, then pour into the pan with the bones. Add the thyme, garlic, and veal stock and bring to a boil. Simmer for 45 minutes, skimming occasionally, then strain.

MAKES ABOUT 2 QUARTS

2 lb beef bones or lean
  trimmings, chopped
  small
1 onion, peeled and sliced
¾ cup dry white wine
2 sprigs of thyme
2 garlic cloves
2½ quarts veal stock
  (see page 322)

Jus de veau

VEAL JUS

Preheat the oven to 425°F. Put the bones in a roasting pan and roast them in the oven, turning occasionally, until brown all over. Transfer the bones to a deep saucepan.

Brown the shallots in the roasting pan, stirring frequently. Add the wine and stir to loosen all the residue. Boil to reduce by half, then pour into the saucepan with the bones. Add the stock and bring to a boil. Simmer for 45 minutes, skimming occasionally, then strain.

MAKES ABOUT 2 QUARTS

2 lb veal bones, chopped small
3 shallots, chopped
¾ cup dry white wine
2½ quarts veal stock (see page 322)

Jus de gibier

GAME JUS

Preheat the oven to 425°F. Put the bones in a roasting pan and roast them in the oven, turning occasionally, until brown all over. Transfer the bones to a deep saucepan.

Brown the shallots in the roasting pan, stirring frequently. Add the Madeira and juniper berries and stir to loosen all the residue. Boil to reduce by half, then pour into the saucepan with the bones. Add the stock and bring to a boil. Simmer for 45 minutes, skimming occasionally, then strain.

MAKES ABOUT 2 QUARTS

2 lb game bird bones, chopped small
3 shallots, chopped
¾ cup Madeira wine
5 juniper berries, crushed
2 quarts chicken stock (see page 320)

Jus d'agneau

LAMB JUS

Preheat the oven to 425°F. Put the bones in a roasting pan and roast them in the oven, turning occasionally, until brown all over. Transfer the bones to a deep saucepan.

Brown the onion in the roasting pan, stirring frequently. Add the wine and stir to loosen all the caramelized bits on the bottom of the pan. Boil to reduce by half, then pour into the saucepan with the bones. Add the thyme, garlic, and veal stock and bring to a boil. Simmer for 45 minutes, skimming occasionally, then strain.

MAKES ABOUT 2 QUARTS

2 lb lamb bones, chopped small
1 onion, sliced
1 cup dry white wine
2 sprigs of thyme
2 garlic cloves
2½ quarts veal stock

Sauce Hollandaise

HOLLANDAISE SAUCE

Boil the vinegar in a small pan with the peppercorns and salt, then take the pan off the heat. Add 2 tablespoons water and the egg yolks, transfer the mixture to a double boiler (not too hot) or a bowl set over a pan of simmering water, and whisk until the egg yolks are light and creamy, 8–10 minutes. Don't let the mixture get too hot, or the egg yolks will scramble.

Take the mixture off the heat and pour in the clarified butter (see below), whisking continuously. Pass the sauce through a fine sieve and add a little lemon juice to taste.

CLARIFIED BUTTER

Melt the butter in a small pan over low heat until it foams. Spoon off the foam and let the butter settle. Remove the clarified butter with a ladle, discarding the whitish residue in the base of the pan.

MAKES ⅔ CUP

2 tsp white wine vinegar
1 tsp cracked white
   peppercorns
pinch salt
4 free-range egg yolks
⅞ cup unsalted butter,
   clarified
lemon juice, to taste

Sauce Béarnaise

BÉARNAISE SAUCE

Put the shallots in a pan with the tarragon, vinegar, peppercorns, and 1 tablespoon water and boil to reduce by half. Remove from the heat and let cool. When cold, add the egg yolks and whisk the mixture in a double boiler – or in a bowl set over a pan of simmering water – until the yolks are light and creamy, 8–10 minutes. Don't let the mixture get too hot, or the eggs will scramble.

Take the mixture off the heat and gently pour in the clarified butter, whisking constantly. Season with a little salt and add the fresh snipped chervil before serving.

SAUCE PALOISE

Use fresh mint instead of tarragon and chervil. Delicious with grilled lamb.

SAUCE CHORON

Peel, deseed, and chop 5 ripe plum tomatoes and sweat them in a little butter to remove the excess moisture. Add to the finished Béarnaise sauce.

MAKES ¾ CUP

2 shallots, peeled and finely chopped

3 tbsp snipped fresh tarragon

3 tbsp white wine vinegar or tarragon vinegar

1 tsp crushed white peppercorns

4 free-range egg yolks

1 cup unsalted butter, clarified (*opposite*)

2 tbsp snipped fresh chervil

salt

Beurre blanc

BUTTER SAUCE

Put the wine, vinegar, and shallots in a heavy-bottomed saucepan. Bring to a boil and continue to cook until the liquid is reduced by half. Add the cream and boil for 1 minute, then lower the heat and gradually whisk in the cubes of cold butter.

I like to keep the shallots in the sauce, but if you prefer a smoother finish, pass the sauce through a fine sieve. Season with salt and pepper to taste.

MAKES ABOUT 1¼ CUPS

6 tbsp dry white wine
1 tbsp white wine vinegar
2 shallots, peeled and finely chopped
¼ cup heavy cream
⅞ cups cold unsalted butter, cubed
salt
black pepper

Mayonnaise

Put the egg yolks, mustard, salt, and vinegar in a round-bottomed bowl and mix with a balloon whisk until smooth. Gradually pour in all the oil in a steady stream, whisking continuously until the mixture is rich and creamy.

This can be kept in a covered container in the fridge for up to a week.

MAKES ABOUT 2½ CUPS

2 free-range egg yolks
1 tbsp Dijon mustard
1 tsp fine salt
½ tbsp white wine vinegar
2 cups vegetable oil
¼ cup extra-virgin olive oil

Mayonnaise aux herbes

HERB MAYONNAISE

Put all the ingredients except the oil in a blender and blitz. With the blender on full speed, slowly pour in the oil.

MAKES ABOUT 1 CUP

2 free-range egg yolks
½ tbsp Dijon mustard
1 tbsp tarragon vinegar
6 tbsp chopped fresh herbs
  (chives, tarragon, flat-leaf
  parsley, dill)
1 tsp salt
black pepper
1 generous cup vegetable oil

Aïoli

GARLIC MAYONNAISE

Slice the garlic lengthwise, removing any green shoots, then put it in a blender with the egg yolks, mustard, vinegar, salt, and cayenne pepper, and blend at full speed.

Gradually trickle in the olive oil while the blender is running. After half of the oil has been incorporated, stop and scrape down the sides of the blender with a spatula.

Continue to trickle in the oil, scraping the sides of the blender once or twice more, and adding 1–2 tablespoons of cold water with the last of the oil to thin the consistency slightly, until you have a smooth garlic mayonnaise.

MAKES 1 GENEROUS CUP

5 garlic cloves, peeled
2 free-range egg yolks
1 tsp Dijon mustard
2 tsp white wine vinegar
pinch salt
pinch cayenne pepper
1 cup light olive oil
1–2 tbsp cold water

Sauce vin rouge

RED WINE SAUCE

Fry the beef trimmings in a pan with a little olive oil until crisp. Drain off the fat, add the wine and port, and reduce by half, occasionally skimming off the fat and scum that come to the surface.

Heat a little olive oil in another pan and cook the onion, shallots, and bacon until well browned. Add the peppercorns and then pour in the reduced wine, followed by the stock. Bring to a boil and skim, then turn down the heat and simmer for 35 minutes. Pass the sauce through a fine sieve.

To serve with steaks, bring the sauce to a boil and reduce until slightly thickened. Take the pan off the heat and whisk in a little cold butter, cut into small cubes.

MAKES 1½ QUARTS

4 oz beef trimmings
    (bone or sinew)
olive oil
1 bottle of full-bodied red
    wine (Syrah or Shiraz)
6 tbsp port
1 onion, peeled and sliced
2 shallots, peeled and sliced
3 oz smoked bacon, chopped
1 tsp cracked white and black
    peppercorns
2 quarts veal stock
    (see page 322)

Sauce à l'estragon

TARRAGON SAUCE

Melt a tablespoon of the butter in a pan and sweat the shallots over low heat until softened but not colored. When the shallots are soft, deglaze the pan with the tarragon vinegar and wine, then reduce the liquid until the pan is nearly dry.

Pour in the stock and reduce until syrupy. Add the cream and boil for 2 minutes, then whisk in the remaining butter, season to taste, and add the tarragon leaves just before serving with chicken or poached fish. Do not strain this sauce, as the texture of the shallots adds another dimension.

MAKES 1 CUP

2 tbsp unsalted butter
2 shallots, peeled and finely
    chopped
2 tbsp tarragon vinegar
6 tbsp dry white wine
1⅔ cup chicken stock
    (see page 320)
6 tbsp heavy cream
5 tbsp tarragon leaves,
    chopped
salt
white pepper

Vinaigrette aux herbes

HERB DRESSING

Put the egg yolks in a blender with the mustard, vinegar, salt, and pepper. Blend at high speed, slowly adding the olive and vegetable oils a little at a time. After a third of the oil has been incorporated, add the herbs. Continue to blend, adding the oils a little at a time. The vinaigrette should have the consistency of pouring cream. If the mixture becomes too thick, add a few drops of cold water to the blender.

If you want to remove the herbs, pass the vinaigrette through a fine sieve. This can be kept in the fridge for up to 2 weeks.

MAKES ABOUT 2 CUPS

2 free-range egg yolks
1 tsp Dijon mustard
1½ tbsp tarragon vinegar
⅔ cup extra-virgin olive oil
1¼ cups vegetable oil
1 tbsp each of chives,
    flat-leaf parsley, and
    tarragon, chopped
salt
black pepper

Vinaigrette à la tomate

TOMATO DRESSING

Make a tomato "fondue" – peel, seed, and chop 4 ripe tomatoes and cook them in a little olive oil until the mixture is thick and dry.

Make the vinaigrette as above, but replace the herbs with 1 heaping teaspoon of tomato purée and 1 heaping tablespoon of tomato "fondue." Season with a few drops of Tabasco sauce instead of pepper.

MAKES ABOUT 2 CUPS

4 ripe tomatoes
⅔ cup extra-virgin olive oil,
    plus extra for cooking the
    tomatoes
2 free-range egg yolks
1 tsp Dijon mustard
1½ tbsp tarragon vinegar
1 heaping tsp tomato purée
1¼ cups vegetable oil
Tabasco sauce

Gelée au Madère

MADEIRA JELLY

This recipe makes enough Madeira jelly for the ham mousse on page 58. It is also good served with cold meat, especially cured meats and game.

Put the gelatin sheets in a bowl of cold water to soften. Pour the wine into a small pan and bring to boiling point. Immediately take the pan off the heat and whisk in the seasoning and softened gelatin – squeeze out any excess water from the gelatin first. Pass the mixture through a fine sieve, let cool, then chill in the fridge until set.

8 gelatin sheets
1 bottle (750ml) Madeira
  wine
2 tsp salt
1 tsp cracked black pepper

Coulis de tomates

TOMATO PURÉE

Heat the olive oil in a pan and sweat the shallots over __ heat and garlic until soft but not colored. Add the tomato paste and cook for another 3 minutes, then add the sugar, chopped tomatoes, bouquet garni, 2 tablespoons water, and seasoning. Bring to a simmer, cover with a piece of parchment paper, and cook for 20 minutes. Tip everything into a food processor and blend until smooth. Lovely served with spinach soufflés (see page 74).

Any leftover coulis can be kept in the fridge in an airtight container for up to a week and used on pizzas and pasta.

2 tbsp olive oil
2 shallots, peeled and finely
  chopped
3 garlic cloves, peeled and
  finely chopped
1 tbsp tomato paste
1 tbsp sugar
1¾ lb tomatoes, peeled,
  seeded, and chopped
1 bouquet garni
  (see page 342)
salt
black pepper

Chutney de tomates vertes et potiron

GREEN TOMATO AND SQUASH CHUTNEY

Wipe the zucchini clean, then grate it coarsely. Discard the seeds. Chop the tomatoes and put them with the grated squash in a colander. Sprinkle with a very generous amount of sea salt and let drain overnight.

Next day, put all the other ingredients in a large pan and bring them to a boil, then gently press the tomato and squash pulp in a colander to remove as much moisture as possible before adding them to the pan. Simmer until sticky and fragrant, 30–40 minutes.

Pour the chutney into sterilized glass jars and leave them in a cool place to mature for a week before using. This is good with cooked meats or to serve with cheese.

MAKES 3 JARS

1¼ lb zucchini (peeled weight)

1¼ lb green tomatoes, peeled and seeded

1 medium onion, thinly sliced

1 tsp ground black pepper

1½-inch piece fresh root ginger, peeled and grated

1 tsp crushed coriander seeds

¼ tsp ground cloves

1 tbsp tomato paste

1 tsp Madras curry powder

⅔ cup golden raisins

2 cups demerara sugar

2¼ cups (18 fl oz/550ml) white wine vinegar

sea salt

Chutney de tomates aux épices

SPICY TOMATO CHUTNEY

Blanch and skin the tomatoes, then cut them in half, remove the seeds, and chop the flesh roughly. Put the chopped tomatoes in a pan with the ginger, chile, salt, tomato paste, and finely chopped garlic. Simmer over low heat until pulpy.

Add the vinegar, sugar, and raisins and simmer until the mixture thickens. Stir occasionally to prevent it from sticking to the bottom of the pan. Pour the chutney into sterilized glass jars, let cool, and store in the fridge.

MAKES 2 JARS

1⅓ lb ripe red tomatoes

½ tsp ground ginger

1 tsp chili powder

2 tsp salt

2 tsp tomato paste

3 garlic cloves, peeled and finely chopped

½ cup malt vinegar

½ cup light muscovado sugar

⅓ cup raisins

Chips de salsifis

SALSIFY CRISPS

Peel the salsify and slice lengthwise on a mandoline, making the slices as thin as possible. Heat the oil to 350°F in a large pan or a deep-fat fryer. Add the slices of salsify, a few at a time, and deep-fry until crisp. Drain them on paper towels to absorb any excess fat, then serve.

This method can be used to make chips from any root vegetables.

1 salsify
oil, for deep-frying

Chips de pommes

APPLE CRISPS

Preheat the oven to 275°F. Peel the apple – if you use a Granny Smith apple you can leave the skin on – and slice it as thinly as possible. Place the slices in a single layer on a nonstick baking sheet and sprinkle lightly with confectioners' sugar. Place them in the oven until the apple slices have completely dried out, 20 minutes.

Place the warm apple slices on a cold, dry, flat surface. As soon as they are completely cold and set, put them in an airtight container so they stay crisp.

1 apple
1 tbsp confectioners' sugar

Croûtons à l'ail

GARLIC CROUTONS

Thinly slice the baguette. Heat the olive oil in a wide frying pan over medium heat, add the garlic cloves, and cook until they release their aroma. Add the sliced baguette, in batches, and fry gently until golden brown. Drain the croutons on paper towels and season with salt and piment d'Espelette.

For small fried croutons, cut some white bread into ¼-inch cubes or tear it into pieces for a more rustic garnish. Heat enough vegetable oil in a pan to shallow-fry the bread. When the oil is hot and smoking, add the bread with a couple of bruised garlic cloves and a sprig of thyme. Cook until golden, then drain and season lightly with salt.

MAKES ENOUGH FOR 10

1 day-old baguette
1 tbsp olive oil
2 garlic cloves, bruised
ground piment d'Espelette (chile power)
salt

Pâtes à base d'algues

SEAWEED PASTA

Blitz the seaweed with the flour in a food processor to break it down, then add the whole eggs and egg yolks and process again until the mixture comes together in a ball. Tip the mixture out and knead the dough until it is smooth and elastic, then leave it to rest for 20 minutes. Roll the dough out and cut it into strips of the desired size. Cook in salted boiling water.

If you want to make this pasta in advance, roll it out, cut into ribbons and lay it on a surface dusted with semolina. Leave it to dry until needed. Seaweed pasta is good with all seafood.

SERVES 10 AS A GARNISH
OR 4 AS MAIN COURSE

2 oz salted kombu seaweed (rinsed and dried)
4 cups (17 oz) all-purpose flour
3 free-range eggs
5 free-range egg yolks

Crème Chantilly

CHANTILLY CREAM

Whisk the cream with the sugar and vanilla extract, if using, until it forms soft peaks. Serve with pastries, tarts, and other desserts.

If you like, use seeds scraped from a vanilla pod instead of vanilla extract.

¾ cup whipping cream, chilled

¼ cup confectioners' sugar

1 tsp vanilla extract (optional)

Crème pâtissière

CONFECTIONERS' CUSTARD

This is great for filling choux buns, éclairs, or the base of a fruit tart. If you like, you can add a little Chantilly cream to the mixture and flavor it with a liqueur or some vanilla.

Whisk the yolks with the sugar until pale and creamy, then lightly whisk in the flour. Bring the milk to a boil and pour it into the yolk mixture. Stir to mix, then tip the mixture back into the saucepan and bring to a boil, stirring continuously. Boil for about 2 minutes, continuing to stir, then remove from the heat and transfer to a bowl.

MAKES ENOUGH FOR 20 CHOUX BUNS

3 free-range egg yolks

¼ cup superfine sugar

⅓ cup (1½ oz) all-purpose flour, sifted

1 cup milk

Tuiles au miel

HONEY TUILES

These are lovely served with ice cream or for decorating desserts such as panna cotta.

Put the butter, sugar, and honey in a saucepan over low heat until they have melted together. Tip the mixture into a bowl and let cool slightly, then whisk in the flour and egg whites. Chill in the fridge for at least an hour.

Preheat the oven to 350°F. Spread the mixture very thinly on a nonstick baking sheet and bake until pale brown, 8–10 minutes. Cut into rounds while still warm and leave them to cool on a sheet of parchment paper.

MAKES ABOUT 30

9 tbsp unsalted butter
½ cup light brown sugar
1 scant cup flower-scented clear honey
1⅔ cup (7 oz) all-purpose flour
5 free-range egg whites

Coulis de mûres

BLACKBERRY PURÉE

A berry coulis makes a ideal partner for ice cream or fruit desserts, such as the pear charlotte on page 283, and is very easy to make. The honey adds depth of flavor and consistency to the purée.

Blitz the blackberries with the sugar and honey in a food processor. The quantity of sugar needed depends on the ripeness of the fruit, so add a little and taste, before adding the full amount.

10 oz blackberries
½–¾ cup confectioners' sugar
1 tbsp clear honey

Chef's notes

ARTICHOKE

To prepare an artichoke heart, take the artichoke and remove the stem. Remove the outer leaves until you reach the soft yellow leaves. Cut off the top part of the artichoke where you see the slight indentation in these leaves, then trim off a little more to reveal the fibrous choke. Scoop out the choke with a teaspoon. Trim any dark leaves off the base of the artichoke, rub the cut surfaces with a cut lemon, and leave it in a bowl of water and lemon juice while you prepare the rest.

BLANCH

To blanch vegetables, plunge them into a pan of salted boiling water for a brief period, then drain and plunge into iced water. This stops the cooking process and retains the fresh colors of the vegetables.

BOUQUET GARNI

A bouquet garni is a bundle of herbs for adding to soups, casseroles, and other dishes. I vary contents to match the dish, but the classic version contains parsley stalks, bay leaf, thyme, celery, and leek, all tied with string (or a piece of leek) to keep them together while cooking.

BRAISE

To cook food, usually meat, slowly with some liquid in a covered pan.

CONFIT

The word confit comes from the French verb *confire*, which means to preserve. A confit is usually prepared by cooking meat such as duck, goose, or pork in its own fat and storing it in fat. You can buy confit duck and other preparations or make them yourself. Confit garlic and confit potatoes can be cooked in olive oil.

DEGLAZE

To deglaze a pan means to add stock, wine, or other liquid to a hot frying pan or roasting pan in which food has been cooked, and then stir to loosen any sticky bits from the pan. This helps to maximize the flavor of the sauce or gravy.

FLAMBÉ

The process of adding alcohol to a dish and setting it alight to burn off the alcohol content but leave behind the flavor.

JULIENNE

This is a term used in French cookery to describe the cutting of thin strips of vegetables such as carrots. Trim the carrot top and bottom. Cut a slice off one side to make a flat surface and place the carrot down on that surface. Cut another flat surface on one side, then cut the carrot into neat fine slices. Arrange these in a pile and cut them into thin strips, like matchsticks.

LOBSTER

A lobster can be killed by plunging a sharp knife through the head between the eyes. If you prefer a gentler method, put the lobster in the freezer for about 15 minutes. Don't leave it for too long, or the texture of the meat will be spoiled.

NEW-SEASON GARLIC

This is the fresh garlic, sometimes known as green or "wet" garlic, available in spring. It has a milder, more gentle flavor than older bulbs.

PIMENT D'ESPELETTE

This mild, smoky chile comes only from the village of Espelette in the Basque area of France. The chiles are dried and used whole or flaked, or ground into a powder. In 2000, it was classified as AOC (Appellation d'Origine Contrôlée), meaning that the name is protected and the chiles can be grown only in this area. It is available from specialist grocers and internet sites. You can use hot paprika or another variety of chile powder instead, but some kinds may be a little hotter than the Espelette variety, so add with care.

POACH

To cook food such as fish, eggs, or meat very gently in simmering liquid.

REDUCE

To reduce liquid such as stock or sauce, boil or simmer in an open pan so the liquid evaporates by the required amount, intensifying the flavor.

SUPRÊME

This is a French term for a breast of chicken or other poultry. The breast is boned but may have the wing attached.

TRUFFLE

A truffle is a kind of fungus, which grows around the roots of certain trees. They are expensive but have the most wonderful flavor. There are many different types, but my favorite is the black winter truffle *(Tuber melanosporum)*. Black truffles can be cooked, but are often eaten raw – just shave thin slices over a dish.

TURNING VEGETABLES

Turning root vegetables such as carrots and turnips makes for a neat, elegant presentation and ensures that they are the same size and so cook evenly. Peel the vegetables and cut them into chunks about 2 inches long. Carefully pare the sides of each piece to make a barrel shape that slightly tapers at each end.

VENTRÈCHE

This meat comes from fatty pork belly and may be smoked or salted. If you can't get *ventrèche,* pancetta or bacon are good substitutes.

VERJUS

This is a sour juice from unripe grapes and is not fermented. You can find verjus in good delis, but if none is available, you can use light white wine instead.

Index

To Gisele and Emily – food tastes better when I am with you

Thank you all

The making of this book would not have been possible without the professionalism of chef Francesco Dibenedetto, who worked with me and prepared the food for the photographs. I would also like to thank Noemi Guy for her skill at reading my scribbled lines on sauce-stained scrap paper; Cristian Barnett for capturing the taste of the food so perfectly on film; Miranda Harvey for her skillful eye, tips on how to relax a salad and making carrots disappear; Holly Clifton-Brown for the gorgeous illustrations; Polly Webb-Wilson for the beautiful choice of plates and her navigational skills; Jinny Johnson for being as passionate about good food as I am and for making *The French Kitchen* delicious to read; Amanda Harris and Lucie Stericker at Weidenfeld & Nicolson for directing operations with such care and good humour; Gérard – my brother in law – for shooting straight and filling the freezer with game; and my neighbor Annie for the "mucky eggs."

weldonowen

Published in North America by Weldon Owen, Inc.
1045 Sansome Street, San Francisco, CA 94111
www.weldonowen.com

Weldon Owen is a division of **BONNIER**

First published in Great Britain in 2013
by Weidenfeld & Nicolson, an imprint of
Orion Publishing Group Ltd

Text copyright © Michel Roux Jr.
Design and layout © Weidenfeld & Nicolson

Library of Congress Cataloging-in-Publication data is available

ISBN 13: 978-168188060-0
ISBN 10: 168188060-1

Photographer: Cristian Barnett
Illustrator: Holly Clifton-Brown
Stylist: Polly Webb-Wilson

Printed and bound in Italy

FSC
www.fsc.org

MIX
Paper from
responsible sources
FSC® C015829